TEACHER'S PET PUBLICATIONS

LITPLAN TEACHER PACK
for
Freak the Mighty
based on the book by
Rodman Philbrick

Written by
Mary B. Collins & Stacy C. Littleton

© 2007 Teacher's Pet Publications
All Rights Reserved

Copyright Teacher's Pet Publications 2007

Only the student materials in this unit plan (such as worksheets, study questions, and tests) may be reproduced multiple times for use in the purchaser's classroom.

For any additional copyright questions, contact Teacher's Pet Publications.

www.tpet.com

TABLE OF CONTENTS - *Freak The Mighty*

Introduction	5
Unit Objectives	7
Reading Assignment Sheet	8
Unit Outline	9
Study Questions (Short Answer)	13
Quiz/Study Questions (Multiple Choice)	27
Pre-reading Vocabulary Worksheets	49
Lesson One (Introductory Lesson)	69
Oral Reading Evaluation Form	72
Writing Assignment 1	89
Writing Assignment 2	94
Writing Evaluation Form	95
Vocabulary Review Activities	104
Writing Assignment 3	108
Nonfiction Assignment Sheet	106
Extra Writing Assignments/Discussion ?s	100
Unit Review Activities	110
Unit Tests	115
Unit Resource Materials	151
Vocabulary Resource Materials	171

A FEW NOTES ABOUT THE AUTHOR

Rodman Philbrick worked as a longshoreman and boat builder on the New England coast where he grew up. He has been writing since the age of sixteen and has published over a dozen novels, short stories, articles, and reviews.

Freak the Mighty, his first novel for young readers was inspired by a boy who lived a few blocks from his home. *Freak the Mighty* was named an ALA Best Book for Young Adults, a Judy Lopez Memorial Award Honor Book, and an ALA Quick Pick. The book was made into a movie in 1998 by Miramax and released as *The Mighty*.

Other books for young readers include *The Fire Pony, Max the Mighty, REM World, The Last Book In The Universe, The Journal of Douglas Allen Deeds,* and *The Young Man and The Sea.*

Rodman Philbrick and his wife divide their time between Maine and the Florida Keys.

INTRODUCTION

This LitPlan has been designed to develop students' reading, writing, thinking, and language skills through exercises and activities related to *Freak The Mighty*. It includes 21 lessons, supported by extra resource materials.

The **introductory lesson** introduces students to the idea that a person's appearance doesn't necessarily indicate who that person is inside. Following the introductory activity, students are given a transition to explain how the activity relates to the book they are about to read. Following the transition, students are given the materials they will be using during the unit. At the end of the lesson, students begin the pre-reading work for the first reading assignment.

The **reading assignments** are approximately twenty pages each; some are a little shorter while others are a little longer. Students have approximately 15 minutes of pre-reading work to do prior to each reading assignment. This pre-reading work involves reviewing the study questions for the assignment and doing some vocabulary work for 7 to 10 vocabulary words they will encounter in their reading.

The **study guide questions** are fact-based questions; students can find the answers to these questions right in the text. These questions come in two formats: short answer or multiple choice. The best use of these materials is probably to use the short answer version of the questions as study guides for students (since answers will be more complete), and to use the multiple choice version for occasional quizzes.

The **vocabulary work** is intended to enrich students' vocabularies as well as to aid in the students' understanding of the book. Prior to each reading assignment, students will complete a two-part worksheet for approximately 7 to 10 vocabulary words in the upcoming reading assignment. Part I focuses on students' use of general knowledge and contextual clues by giving the sentence in which the word appears in the text. Students are then to write down what they think the words mean based on the words' usage. Part II nails down the definitions of the words by giving students dictionary definitions of the words and having students match the words to the correct definitions based on the words' contextual usage. Students should then have an understanding of the words when they meet them in the text.

After each reading assignment, students will go back and formulate answers for the study guide questions. Discussion of these questions serves as a **review** of the most important events and ideas presented in the reading assignments.

After students complete reading the work, there is a **vocabulary review** lesson which pulls together all of the fragmented vocabulary lists for the reading assignments and gives students a review of all of the words they have studied.

Following the vocabulary review, a lesson is devoted to the **extra discussion questions/writing assignments**. These questions focus on interpretation, critical analysis, and personal response, employing a variety of thinking skills and adding to the students' understanding of the novel.

There is a **group theme project** in this unit. Students will become knights on a quest to bring their Liege information about the Arthurian Legend.

There are three **writing assignments** in this unit, each with the purpose of informing, persuading, or having students express personal opinions. In Writing Assignment One students will write an informative essay about their quest project assignments. Writing Assignment Two asks students to give a personal response to one of two quotes from the story. In Writing Assignment Three students pretend to be the prosecuting attorney for Killer Kane's attempted murder trial, and they write their closing arguments to the jury.

There is a **nonfiction reading assignment.** Students must read nonfiction articles, books, etc. to gather information about their themes in our world today.

The **review lesson** pulls together all of the aspects of the unit. The teacher is given four or five choices of activities or games to use which all serve the same basic function of reviewing all of the information presented in the unit.

The **unit test** comes in two formats: multiple choice or short answer. As a convenience, two different tests for each format have been included. There is also an advanced short answer unit test for advanced students.

There are additional **support materials** included with this unit. The **Unit Resource Materials** section includes suggestions for an in-class library, crossword and word search puzzles related to the novel, and extra worksheets. There is a list of **bulletin board ideas** which gives the teacher suggestions for bulletin boards to go along with this unit. In addition, there is a list of **extra class activities** the teacher could choose from to enhance the unit or as a substitution for an exercise the teacher might feel is inappropriate for his/her class. **Answer keys** are located directly after the **reproducible student materials** throughout the unit. The **Vocabulary Resource Materials** section includes similar worksheets and games to reinforce the vocabulary words.

The **level** of this unit can be varied depending upon the criteria on which the individual assignments are graded, the teacher's expectations of his/her students in class discussions, and the formats chosen for the study guides, quizzes and test. If teachers have other ideas/activities they wish to use, they can usually easily be inserted prior to the review lesson.

The student materials may be reproduced for use in the teacher's classroom without infringement of copyrights. No other portion of this unit may be reproduced without the written consent of Teacher's Pet Publications, Inc.

UNIT OBJECTIVES - *Freak The Mighty*

1. Through reading *Freak The Mighty*, students will explore how disabilities can be overcome with the strength of friendship.

2. Students will demonstrate their understanding of the text on four levels: factual, interpretive, critical, and personal.

3. Students will practice reading orally and silently.

4. Students will study the Arthurian Legend.

5. Students will answer questions to demonstrate their knowledge and understanding of the main events and characters in *Freak The Migthy* as they relate to the author's theme development.

6. Students will enrich their vocabularies and improve their understanding of the novel through the vocabulary lessons prepared for use in conjunction with the novel.

7. The writing assignments in this unit are geared to several purposes:
    a. To have students demonstrate their abilities to inform, to persuade, or to express their own personal ideas
        Note: Students will demonstrate the ability to write effectively to <u>inform</u> by developing and organizing facts to convey information. Students will demonstrate the ability to write effectively to <u>persuade</u> by selecting and organizing relevant information, establishing an argumentative purpose, and by designing an appropriate strategy for an identified audience. Students will demonstrate the ability to write effectively to <u>express personal ideas</u> by selecting a form and its appropriate elements.
    b. To check the students' reading comprehension
    c. To make students think about the ideas presented by the novel
    d. To encourage logical thinking
    e. To provide an opportunity to practice good grammar and improve students' use of the English language.

8. Students will read aloud, report, and participate in large and small group discussions to improve their public speaking and personal interaction skills.

9. Students will read and share non-fiction articles related to the book.

READING ASSIGNMENT SHEET - *Freak The Mighty*

Date Assigned	Chapters Assigned	Completion Date
	1-4	
	5-7	
	8-10	
	11-13	
	14-15	
	16-19	
	20-22	
	23-25	

UNIT OUTLINE - *Freak The Mighty*

1	2	3	4	5
Introduction PV 1-4	R 1-4 LD Exercise	Study ? 1-4 PVR 5-7	Study ? 5-7 Introduction to Quest Project Writing #1	PVR 8-10 Bullies, Gangs, and Terrorists
6 Study ? 8-10 PVR 11-13 Quest Groups	**7** Study? 11-13 PVR 14-15	**8** Study ? 14-15 Quest Projects PVR 16-19	**9** Writing Assignment #2	**10** Study? 16-19 PVR 20-22
11 Study? 20-22 PVR 23-25	**12** Study? 23-25 Themes	**13** Extra Discussion	**14** Extra Discussion Continued	**15** Vocabulary Review
16 Nonfiction	**17** Writing Assignment #3	**18** Quest Presentations	**19** Quest Presentations Continued	**20** Unit Review
21 Unit Test				

Key: P = Preview Study Questions   V = Vocabulary Work   R = Read

STUDY GUIDE QUESTIONS

SHORT ANSWER STUDY GUIDE QUESTIONS - *Freak The Mighty*

Chapters 1 - 4
1. Who is telling the story?
2. Who are Gram and Grim?
3. Max sees Freak for the first time in day care. What does Max think of Freak?
4. Identify *Him*.
5. Why is Grim concerned about Maxwell?
6. What didn't Max have until Freak moved down the street?
7. Describe the down under. Why does Max like the down under?
8. The second time Max sees Freak, he is giving orders to the moving men. Describe how Freak looks when Max sees him.
9. What does Max retrieve from the tree for Freak?
10. What observation does Max make about how Freak talks?
11. What does Freak do and say when Max asks him why he calls his mother "Fair Gwen of Air"?
12. What does Max know about King Arthur?
13. What is Freak's version of the Arthurian Legend?
14. Why is Freak really interested in the knights?
15. What does Freak tell Max about robots?
16. What is Freak's mother's reaction to seeing Max?

Chapters 5 - 7
1. Describe how Max feels when he goes to the place in his head.
2. What was Gwen's relationship with Max's mother?
3. What does Gwen think of Max's father?
4. People say that Max is the "spitting image" of his father. Why is it bad for Max to look like his father?
5. Why does Max cry like a baby when he goes to bed after having dinner with Freak and Gwen?
6. What happens to Max and Freak when they are walking to the millpond to see the fireworks?
7. Identify Blade.
8. Why does Max put Freak on his shoulders at the fireworks display?
9. Describe what happens to Freak and Max after the fireworks.
10. How do Freak and Max get out of the pond after escaping from Tony D. and his gang?
11. After rescuing Freak and Max from the pond muck, who does the cop say Max is?
12. When the police officers ask for the boys' names after rescuing them, what name does Kevin give the police?

Freak the Mighty Short Answer Study Questions Page 2

Chapters 8 - 10
1. How do Grim and Gram react to Max's being a hero?
2. What does Max think about rescuing Freak?
3. What does Gram ask Max to do with regards to the hoodlum boy? What is his response?
4. What has become a habit for Max and Freak when they go out together?
5. What secret does Max promise to keep about the Medical Research building?
6. What does Freak tell Max when he asks if the transplant will hurt and if it is dangerous?
7. What is the quest Freak and Max have to wait until exactly three in the morning to do?
8. What is the treasure in the storm drain?
9. How did the treasure get into the storm drain?

Chapters 11 - 13
1. What does Max call the New Tenements?
2. What type of people live in the Testaments?
3. Identify Loretta Lee.
4. Why does Max like Freak riding on his shoulders?
5. What does Max know about Iggy?
6. Why does Iggy let Max and Freak leave without messing with them?
7. What does Freak tell Max about his father's leaving after he was born?
8. Why does Gram agree to sign the papers allowing Max to be in the smart classes?
9. What happens in Mrs. Donelli's class that gets Max and Freak sent to the principal's office?
10. What does Freak teach Max that no one else has been able to do?
11. How is reading different from writing to Max?
12. Why does Max think Mrs. Addison has called him to the office?
13. What does Mrs. Addison promise Max regarding his father?
14. What happens to Freak while Max is getting him more chop suey?

Chapters 14 - 16
1. Why does Freak **not** want Gwen to hear Max talking about the robot stuff?
2. Why does Freak need a new body?
3. While Max is in the down under wrapping Christmas presents he hears shouting. Why are Gram and Grim shouting?
4. What does Grim tell Max about his father?
5. On Christmas Eve what do Freak, Max, Grim, Gram, and Gwen do?
6. Describe the box and gift Freak gives to Max Christmas Eve. What does Max think of his gift from Freak?
7. What happens to Max in the night on Christmas Eve?
8. What does Max's father tell him is the truth?
9. What has Max always feared about his father?
10. Where does Killer Kane take Max on Christmas Eve?

Freak the Mighty Short Answer Study Questions Page 3

Chapters 17 - 19
1. Where does Iggy take Max and Killer Kane on Christmas Eve?
2. What does Killer Kane want Max to know?
3. What does Killer Kane swear on the Bible?
4. What is Killer Kane's plan for the future?
5. Describe where Killer Kane takes Max to hide from the cops.
6. Who first comes to help Max escape from his father?
7. What is the escape plan Loretta describes to Max?
8. What happens while Loretta is untying Max?

Chapters 20 - 22
1. What does Max do to help Loretta?
2. What does Max remember as he sees his father strangling Loretta?
3. How does Killer Kane react to Max's memory about his mother's death?
4. What did Max do when he was four that cost Killer Kane years?
5. Why does Max's father try to strangle him?
6. Who comes to rescue Max and Loretta from Killer Kane?
7. How do Freak and Max get away from Killer Kane?
8. What does everyone say will happen to Killer Kane?
9. What do the newspapers call Loretta Lee?
10. What does Freak tell Max Dr. Spivak says about his unique medical status?
11. What is different about school after Christmas vacation?
12. What happens to Killer Kane?
13. Max is still upset about being like his father. What does Grim say to Max?
14. While walking home on the last day of school what does Freak tell Max about remembering?
15. Why is Freak's birthday like two birthdays?
16. What happens to Freak on his birthday?

Freak the Mighty Short Answer Study Questions Page 4

Chapters 23-25
1. What does Max take to the hospital? Why?
2. Who finds Max outside the hospital, and where is he taken?
3. Describe what Max sees and feels in the ICU.
4. What does Freak tell Max about The Bionic Unit?
5. Freak gives Max a book. What does he tell Max to do with it?
6. What happens when Freak starts coughing in the ICU?
7. What does Max do with the book from Freak?
8. What does Max find out when he gets to the ICU?
9. What does Dr. Spivak tell Max when he says she lied to Freak about his new bionic body?
10. How does Freak die?
11. What does Max do after Freak dies? How does Max feel?
12. What does Grim tell Max about living and having Freak as a friend?
13. How does Max feel when he goes back to school?
14. What does Tony D. say to Max when he returns to school? What does Max do?
15. Who does Max see that winter after Freak dies, and what does she say to him?
16. What does Max do with the empty book?

ANSWER KEY SHORT ANSWER STUDY GUIDE QUESTIONS - Freak The Mighty

Chapters 1 - 4

1. Who is telling the story?
   Maxwell is the narrator of the story.

2. Who are Gram and Grim?
   Gram is Maxwell's grandmother, and Grim is his grandfather; both are on his mother's side of the family.

3. Max sees Freak for the first time in day care. What does Max think of Freak?
   He thinks Freak is fierce, but he thinks Freak's crutches are cool and the leg braces are even more cool.

4. Identify *Him*.
   Max's grandparents refer to Max's father as *Him*.

5. Why is Grim concerned about Maxwell?
   He is concerned because Maxwell looks like his father and is afraid Max will inherit his father's character.

6. What didn't Max have until Freak moved down the street?
   Max did not have a brain until Freak moved down the street.

7. Describe the down under. Why does Max like the down under?
   The down under is a little room Grim built in the basement for Max. The paneling buckles in a regular ripple effect, and the carpet smells like low tide. He has the place to himself with no fear of Gram sticking her head in the door, asking what he is doing.

8. The second time Max sees Freak, he is giving orders to the moving men. Describe how Freak looks when Max sees him.
   ". . . he's got a normal-sized head, but the rest of him is shorter than a yardstick and kind of twisted in a way that means he can't stand up and makes his chest puff out . . . ."

9. What does Max retrieve from the tree for Freak?
   It is a plastic bird, light as a feather. Freak calls the plastic bird an ornithopter.

10. What observation does Max make about how Freak talks?
    Max says Freak talks ". . . like right out of a dictionary. So smart you can hardly believe it."

11. What does Freak do and say when Max asks him why he calls his mother "Fair Gwen of Air"?

    Max notices that Freak tries not to show he is laughing inside. Freak shakes his head and tells Max his mother's name is Gwen, so he calls her the Fair Guinevere or the Fair Gwen after Guinevere, from the legend of King Arthur.

12. What does Max know about King Arthur?

    King Arthur is a brand of flour Gram uses.

13. What is Freak's version of the Arthurian Legend?

    "King Arthur was the first king of England, way back when there were still dragons and monsters in the world. Arthur was this wimpy little kid, an orphan, and there was this magic sword stuck in a big stone. The old king died, and whoever could pull the sword from the stone proved he was the next king. All these big tough dudes came from all over to yank at the sword and they couldn't budge it. One day this wimpy little kid tried it when nobody was looking and the sword slipped out like it was stuck in butter."

14. Why is Freak really interested in the knights?

    He believes the knights were like the first human version of robots. Hundreds of years before they had computers they were already attempting to exceed the design limitations of the human body.

15. What does Freak tell Max about robots?

    Robots are not just in the movies. Robotics, the science of designing and building functional robots, is a huge industry.

16. What is Freak's mother's reaction to seeing Max?

    She appears to be scared of Max.

<u>Chapters 5 - 7</u>

1. Describe how Max feels when he goes to the place in his head.

    He is floating, it's cool and empty. He feels like nothing, like nobody, like nothing matters.

2. What was Gwen's relationship with Max's mother?

    Max's mother and Gwen were good friends before she got married.

3. What does Gwen think of Max's father?

    Gwen thinks he is crazy and scary.

4. People say that Max is the "spitting image" of his father. Why is it bad for Max to look like his father?

    Everyone in town knows his father is in prison and why he is there.

5. Why does Max cry like a baby when he goes to bed after having dinner with Freak and Gwen?
    Max cries because he is happy.

6. What happens to Max and Freak when they are walking to the millpond to see the fireworks?
    Tony D. and his gang stop them and harass them. They are "saved" when the gang members run away when a police car drives nearby.

7. Identify Blade.
    Blade is Tony D.'s nickname. He is seventeen and has been to juvenile court three or four times.

8. Why does Max put Freak on his shoulders at the fireworks display?
    There are so many people around, all Freak can see are feet and knees. People are lifting their little kids up to see the fireworks explode, so Max sort of reaches down without thinking and picks up Freak and puts him on his shoulders.

9. Describe what happens to Freak and Max after the fireworks.
    Tony D. and his gang again come after Freak and Max. Because he is up high, Freak can see who is coming after them and where they are. He directs Max, who is running with Freak on his shoulders, by kicking him on the right or left. Freak directs Max into the millpond, where they escape but get stuck in the mud.

10. How do Freak and Max get out of the pond after escaping from Tony D. and his gang?
    Freak sees a police car and whistles loudly to get the officers' attention. The police use ropes to pull Max out.

11. After rescuing Freak and Max from the pond muck, who does the cop say Max is?
    He identifies Max as Kenny (Killer) Kane's boy.

12. When the police officers ask for the boys' names after rescuing them, what name does Kevin give the police?
    He says they are "Freak the Mighty."

<u>Chapters 8 - 10</u>
1. How do Grim and Gram react to Max's being a hero?
    Gram makes a fuss over him, and when Max asks if he could have sugar for his coffee, Grim says, "Of course you can, son." Max has proved himself to be a "good guy," so Grim finally accepts him.

2. What does Max think about rescuing Freak?
    He thinks he did not rescue Freak; rather, Freak rescued him with his genius brain.

3. What does Gram ask Max to do with regards to the hoodlum boy? What is his response?
>She wants Max to promise her he will keep away from him. Max tells her he will run.

4. What has become a habit for Max and Freak when they go out together?
>Freak rides up high on Max's shoulders and uses his little feet to steer Max if he forgets where they are going.

5. What secret does Max promise to keep about the Medical Research building?
>Inside is a secret laboratory called The Experimental Bionics Unit. At some future time Freak will enter the lab and become the first bionically improved human.

6. What does Freak tell Max when he asks if the transplant will hurt and if it is dangerous?
>Freak says, "Sure it will hurt. Life is dangerous."

7. What is the quest Freak and Max have to wait until exactly three in the morning to do?
>The quest is a treasure hunt, only it's not really a hunt because Freak knows the "treasure" is in a storm drain.

8. What is the treasure in the storm drain?
>The treasure is a purse belonging to Loretta Lee.

9. How did the treasure get into the storm drain?
>Freak tells Max he saw one of Tony D.'s punks stuff it in the sewer.

Chapters 11 - 13

1. What does Max call the New Tenements?
>He calls them the New Testaments or just the Testaments. He has the words confused with a section of the Bible.

2. What type of people live in the Testaments?
>Poor people and drug addicts live there.

3. Identify Loretta Lee.
>The "treasure" purse Max and Freak find in the storm drain belongs to her. She lives in the New Tenements with Iggy. She knew Killer Kane and Freak's mom, Gwen.

4. Why does Max like Freak riding on his shoulders?
>He likes having a really smart brain on his shoulders, helping him think.

5. What does Max know about Iggy?
>He is the boss of The Panheads, a bad-news motorcycle gang.

6. Why does Iggy let Max and Freak leave without messing with them?
   He did not want to take the chance that Killer Kane would find out he was messing with his kid.

7. What does Freak tell Max about his father's leaving after he was born?
   Freak said his mother won't talk about it. All she says is, "He made his decision and I made mine." "But I know he ran away because of me. Good riddance to bad rubbish."

8. Why does Gram agree to sign the papers allowing Max to be in the smart classes?
   Grim asks her to give it a try since nothing else has worked. He thinks that maybe Max just needs a friend.

9. What happens in Mrs. Donelli's class that gets Max and Freak sent to the principal's office?
   The class makes fun of Max and Freak, chanting "Killer Kane! Killer Kane! Had a kid who got no brain!" Freak climbs onto Max's shoulders, rasing his fists and punching the air calling out, "Freak the Mighty! Freak the Mighty!" Then the entire class starts chanting, "Freak the Mighty!"

10. What does Freak teach Max that no one else has been able to do?
    Freak has been showing Max how to read a whole book, and it all makes sense.

11. How is reading different from writing to Max?
    ". . . reading is just a way of listening, and [he] could always listen, but writing is like talking, and that's a whole other ball game."

12. Why does Max think Mrs. Addison has called him to the office?
    Max thinks Mrs. Addison is going to put him back in the learning disabled class.

13. What does Mrs. Addison promise Max regarding his father?
    Mrs. Addison promises Max he would not have to do anything he did not want to. She tells him she will make it very clear to the parole board and to his father's lawyer.

14. What happens to Freak while Max is getting him more chop suey?
    When Max comes back, something is wrong, Freak's face is all red and swollen up and he is making this huk-huk-huk noise. Freak chokes on the chop suey.

Chapters 14 - 16

1. Why does Freak **not** want Gwen to hear Max talking about the robot stuff?
   Freak said The Fair Gwen must not know of the plan because the very idea strikes fear in her heart.

2. Why does Freak need a new body?
   Freak is growing on the inside but not on the outside.

3. While Max is in the down under wrapping Christmas presents he hears shouting. Why are Gram and Grim shouting?
    Grim wants to get a gun to protect his family, but Gram doesn't want a gun in the house.

4. What does Grim tell Max about his father?
    Grim tells Max his father is up for parole, but he has gone to court and made it so Max's father won't be allowed within a mile of the house.

5. On Christmas Eve what do Freak, Max, Grim, Gram, and Gwen do?
    On Christmas Eve they all have dinner and pretend everything is normal, no one says a word about Killer Kane.

6. Describe the box and gift Freak gives to Max Christmas Eve. What does Max think of his gift from Freak?
    The box is pointed at the top like a pyramid and wrapped in Sunday comics. When the paper is off there are arrows all over directing Max to a sign that says PRESS HERE AND BE AMAZED. After Max presses the spot all four sides fold down at the same time. Inside the box is a dictionary that Freak had written for Max. Max thinks the dictionary is the best. Everything else is extra.

7. What happens to Max in the night on Christmas Eve?
    His father sneaks into his room and tells Max, "I came back like I promised."
    Killer Kane clamps his hand over Max's mouth. Max feels paralyzed and his head is empty and all there is in the world is a big hand and cool breath like the wind.

8. What does Max's father tell him is the truth?
    He says he never killed anybody, and that is the truth.

9. What has Max always feared about his father?
    Max always knew his father would come for him in the night, that he would wake up to find him there, filling the room, and that would make him feel empty.

10. Where does Killer Kane take Max on Christmas Eve?
    He takes Max to Iggy and Loretta's apartment in the New Testaments.

<u>Chapters 17 - 19</u>
1. Where does Iggy take Max and Killer Kane on Christmas Eve?
    Iggy takes them down a back alley to a door that has been busted open and down a dark hallway. The apartment they go in belongs to an old woman who has gone to visit her sister for the holidays.

2. What does Killer Kane want Max to know?
    One thing is that he never killed anybody. The other is that he sent presents and letters to Max from prison, which Max's grandparents never gave him.

3. What does Killer Kane swear on the Bible?
    "I, Kenneth David Kane, do swear by all that's Holy that I did not murder this boy's mother. And if that isn't the truth, may God strike me dead."

4. What is Killer Kane's plan for the future?
    Killer Kane tells Max they will get a big impressive RV and put a sign on the side: The Reverend Kenneth David Kane or another name to be on the safe side. Then Max will stand out in front of the bus in a real nice suit collecting money in a basket. Max won't have to steal the money because folks love to give to a man of God. Killer Kane will preach, he says people love to hear about a bad man who has redeemed himself.

5. Describe where Killer Kane takes Max to hide from the cops.
    He takes Max on the other side of the alley to a boarded-up building that used to be part of the Testaments until a fire burned it out. Everything is black and wet, and old pipes and wires are hanging down. Everywhere under foot is broken glass the color of smoke.

6. Who first comes to help Max escape from his father?
    Loretta Lee comes to help Max.

7. What is the escape plan Loretta describes to Max?
    Loretta tells Max that Iggy will keep Killer Kane busy while she gets Max loose. She also tells him that there are enough cops out there to start war, and they will be safe when they get out of this godforsaken place.

8. What happens while Loretta is untying Max?
    Two big hands are squeezing her neck. Max sees his father come out of the darkness and it is his hands around her throat, shoving her back.

Chapters 20 - 22
1. What does Max do to help Loretta?
    Max's hands and feet are numb and he can hardly walk, so all he can do is sort of fall on top of Killer Kane and try to shove him loose from her.

2. What does Max remember as he sees his father strangling Loretta?
    He remembers seeing his father killing his mother.

3. How does Killer Kane react to Max's memory about his mother's death?
    He tells Max he was only four years old and that he could not possibly recall that event.

4. What did Max do when he was four that cost Killer Kane years?
    After killing his mother, Killer Kane locked Max in his bedroom. Max ran to the window and broke it with his hand and started yelling for someone to come and help Mommy.

5. Why does Max's father try to strangle him?
   He realizes Max really does remember seeing him kill Max's mother. He thinks he has to "clean this mess up" and get rid of Max, the witness to both the murder of Max's mother and his attempted murder of Loretta.

6. Who comes to rescue Max and Loretta from Killer Kane?
   Freak comes to the rescue.

7. How do Freak and Max get away from Killer Kane?
   Freak has a squirt gun he tells Killer Kane is filled with sulfuric acid. Freak sprays Killer Kane right in the eyes. While Killer Kane is screaming and scrubbing at his eyes, Max picks up Freak and goes running through the dark toward the stairs.

8. What does everyone say will happen to Killer Kane?
   Everyone keeps saying that this time they've got Killer Kane where they want him, for violation of parole, violation of a restraining order, abduction of a minor, and two counts of attempted murder. This time they will lock him up for good.

9. What do the newspapers call Loretta Lee?
   The papers call Loretta the Heroic Biker Babe.

10. What does Freak tell Max Dr. Spivak says about his unique medical status?
    Dr. Spivak says Freak's unique status as a marvel of genetic aberration makes him an object of intense curiosity. Specialists from the world over are familiar with his case.

11. What is different about school after Christmas vacation?
    School is different because everyone is jealous Max and Freak got their picture in the papers. Mrs. Donelli calls them "the dynamic duo" and puts the picture from the paper on the bulletin board.

12. What happens to Killer Kane?
    Just before the trial starts, Killer Kane pleads guilty. He makes a deal to serve out the rest of his original sentence plus ten more years.

13. Max is still upset about being like his father. What does Grim say to Max?
    "The man is an accident of nature," he says. "All you got from him is your looks and your size. You've got your mother's heart, and that's what counts."

14. While walking home on the last day of school what does Freak tell Max about remembering?
    Freak says, "Remembering is just an invention of the mind."

15. Why is Freak's birthday like two birthdays?
    Freak's birthday is like two because not only is it Freak's birthday, Freak the Mighty is almost a year old, too.

16. What happens to Freak on his birthday?
   Freak has a seizure and is taken to the hospital.

Chapters 23-25
1. What does Max take to the hospital? Why?
   Max takes the old ornithopter bird, figuring maybe Freak will get a chance to look out the window and see it flittering by.

2. Who finds Max outside the hospital, and where is he taken?
   Gwen finds Max and takes him to see Freak, because Freak is insisting on seeing him.

3. Describe what Max sees and feels in the ICU.
   There are so many nurses he can't hardly turn around without bumping in to one. There is all this electronic gear Gwen says is called telemetry. Max is not scared until he sees Freak and how small he looks on the bed with tubes going into his arms and up his nose.

4. What does Freak tell Max about The Bionic Unit?
   Freak tells Max The Bionic Unit is on red alert. That tonight they will take him down there for his special operation and that the next time Max sees him he will be new and improved.

5. Freak gives Max a book. What does he tell Max to do with it?
   Freak gives Max a book with all the pages blank. Freak tells Max to fill it with their adventures.

6. What happens when Freak starts coughing in the ICU?
   When Freak starts coughing the doctor and nurses are swarming all over the room and Dr. Spivak tells Max to leave.

7. What does Max do with the book from Freak?
   Max put the book in the pyramid box for safekeeping and for good luck.

8. What does Max find out when he gets to the ICU?
   Max finds out that Freak has died. He notices that some of the nurses are crying and looking at him strange, and all of a sudden he goes nuts.

9. What does Dr. Spivak tell Max when he says she lied to Freak about his new bionic body?
   She told Max, "You know better than that, Maxwell. You couldn't lie to Kevin. I tried a little fib on him when he was about seven years old, because I didn't think a child could handle the whole truth, and you know what he did? He looked his disease up in a medical dictionary."

10. How does Freak die?
    Dr. Spivak tells Max that Freak's heart just got too big for his body.

11. What does Max do after Freak dies? How does Max feel?
    Max hides in the down under, which is why he misses the funeral and the Fair Gwen's going away. Max feels like a balloon and somebody has let all the air out. He doesn't care if the air comes back because "it doesn't matter if you are going to die in the end."

12. What does Grim tell Max about living and having Freak as a friend?
    Grim tells Max it isn't how long you have, but what you do with the time you have. He told him he should count himself lucky because most of us go through life and never have a friend like Kevin.

13. How does Max feel when he goes back to school?
    Max hated every minute, especially how people kept feeling sorry for him, as if he was the one who died.

14. What does Tony D. say to Max when he returns to school? What does Max do?
    Tony D. tells Max it is a shame what happened. Max blows up and tells him if he ever felt sorry for him again, he'd put him headfirst in the millpond and pound him down into the mud like a fence post.

15. Who does Max see that winter after Freak dies, and what does she say to him?
    Max sees Loretta. When she asks him what he is doing, he says, "Nothing." She gives him a long look and says, "Nothing is a drag, kid. Think about it."

16. What does Max do with the empty book?
    Max writes *Freak the Mighty*.

STUDY GUIDE/QUIZ QUESTIONS - *Freak The Mighty*
Multiple Choice Format

<u>Chapters 1 - 4</u>

1. Who is telling the story?
    A. Kevin is the narrator of the story.
    B. Maxwell is the narrator of the story.
    C. Gwen is the narrator of the story.
    D. Killer Kane is the narrator of the story.

2. Who are Gram and Grim?
    A. Writers of the Grim's Fairy Tales
    B. Maxwell's foster parents
    C. Maxwell's grandparents, his mother's people, *her* parents
    D. Maxwell's grandparents, his father's people, *his* parents

3. Max sees Freak for the first time in day care. What does Max think of Freak?
    A. Max thinks Freak is a sad little kid.
    B. Max thinks Freak is fierce; he thinks his crutches and leg braces are cool.
    C. Max thinks Freak is bossy.
    D. Max thinks Freak is trying to impress the other kids.

4. Identify *Him*.
    A. Tony D.
    B. Max's father
    C. Grim
    D. Kevin's father

5. Why is Grim concerned about Maxwell?
    A. Grim is concerned because Maxwell looks like his father and is afraid Max will inherit his father's character.
    B. Grim is concerned because Maxwell cannot read.
    C. Grim is concerned because Maxwell spends too much time in the basement.
    D. Grim is concerned because Maxwell has no friends.

6. What didn't Max have until Freak moved down the street?
    A. Max did not have a complaint.
    B. Max did not have a reading coach.
    C. Max did not have an American Flyer wagon.
    D. Max did not have a brain.

Freak The Mighty Multiple Choice Questions Chapters 1 - 4 page 2

7. Describe the down under. Why does Max like the down under?
    A. The down under is the prison where Max's father is; Max likes it because he knows his father cannot break out.
    B. The down under is an old, run-down playground by the millpond where Max likes to daydream.
    C. The down under is a little room Grim built in the basement for Max; he likes it because he has it all to himself.
    D. The down under is the basement in the Testaments; he likes digging through the trash to find cans to sell.

8. The second time Max sees Freak, he is giving orders to the moving men. Describe how Freak looks when Max sees him.
    A. He is short with a small head and big ears.
    B. He has a normal-sized head, but the rest of his body is shorter than a yardstick.
    C. He is tall for his age with a small head.
    D. He has long legs, a short body, and normal-sized head.

9. What does Max retrieve from the tree for Freak?
    A. It is a plastic bird.
    B. It is a football.
    C. It is a flag.
    D. It is a kite.

10. What observation does Max make about how Freak talks?
    A. Freak talks like a robot.
    B. Freak talks like he is King Author.
    C. Freak talks like he is better than Max.
    D. Freak talks like a dictionary.

11. What does Freak do and say when Max asks him why he calls his mother "Fair Gwen of Air"?
    A. Freak tries not to show he is laughing inside and explains to Max that his mother's name is "Gwen," so he calls her the "Fair Gwen" or the "Fair Guinevere" after Guinevere, from the legend of King Arthur.
    B. Freak falls down laughing because he can not believe Max would actually think he calls his mother "Fair Gwen of Air."
    C. Freak just laughs at Max and doesn't say anything.
    D. Freak calls his mother and tells her that Max has given her a new nickname, the "Fair Gwen of Air."

Freak The Mighty Multiple Choice Questions Chapters 1 - 4 page 3

12. What does Max know about King Arthur?
    A. King Arthur created the Round Table.
    B. King Arthur is a brand of flour Gram uses.
    C. King Arthur was the King of England.
    D. King Arthur pulled a magical sword out of a stone.

13. Which is **not** Freak's version of the Arthur Legend?
    A. King Arthur was the first king of England.
    B. There were dragons and monsters in the world when Arthur was king.
    C. Arthur was this wimpy little kid, an orphan.
    D. There was a magic crown stuck in a big stone.

14. Why is Freak really interested in the knights?
    A. He believes the knights were the bravest men who ever lived.
    B. He believes the knights were like the first human version of robots.
    C. He wants to start a club, Freak's Knights of the Round Table.
    D. He thinks everyone should be loyal like the knights.

15. What does Freak tell Max about robots?
    A. Robotics, the science of designing and building functional robots, is a huge industry.
    B. The only real robots are the ones used on car assembly lines.
    C. Robots are only toys.
    D. Robotics, the science of designing and building functional robots, is only real in the movies.

16. What is Freak's mother's reaction to seeing Max?
    A. She is happy to see Max again.
    B. She seems scared of Max.
    C. She tells Freak never to play with Max.
    D. She is surprised.

Freak The Mighty Multiple Choice Questions Chapters 5 - 7

Chapters 5 - 7
1. Describe how Max feels when he goes to the place in his head.
    A. He feels like he can do anything; he feels like he is somebody.
    B. He is sad and lonely; he feels he is the only person in the world.
    C. He is flying; he feels free and happy.
    D. He is floating; it is cool and empty; he feels like nothing, like nobody.

2. What was Gwen's relationship with Max's mother?
    A. Max's mother and Gwen were sisters.
    B. Max's mother and Gwen were enemies high school.
    C. Max's mother and Gwen were good friends before she got married.
    D. Gwen never knew Max's mother.

3. What does Gwen think of Max's father?
    A. Gwen thinks he is crazy and scary.
    B. Gwen thinks he should be with Max.
    C. Gwen thinks he is a lot of fun to be with.
    D. Gwen thinks he should never get out of prison.

4. People say that Max is the "spitting image" of his father. Why is it bad for Max to look like his father?
    A. His father is scary-looking.
    B. Everyone in town knows his father is in prison and why.
    C. People always stare at him.
    D. His father's picture is on a "wanted" poster.

5. Why does Max cry like a baby when he goes to bed after having dinner with Freak and Gwen?
    A. Max cries because he is happy.
    B. Max cries because he is afraid of Freak.
    C. Max cries because Gwen told him he looks just like his father.
    D. Max cries because Gram told him he could not play with Freak again.

6. What happens to Max and Freak when they are walking to the millpond to see the fireworks?
    A. They get lost and miss the fireworks.
    B. They are stopped and harassed by Tony D. and his gang.
    C. Max falls down and lands on Freak, hurting his leg.
    D. They find money on the street and stop to buy candy.

Freak The Mighty Multiple Choice Questions Chapters 5 - 7 page 2

7. Identify Blade.
   A. Blade is a nickname for Killer Kane, Max's father.
   B. Blade is the name of King Arthur's sword.
   C. Blade is a nickname for Iggy, the leader of The Pinheads.
   D. Blade is Tony D.; he is seventeen and has been to juvenile court three or four times.

8. Why does Max put Freak on his shoulders at the fireworks display?
   A. Max puts Freak on his shoulders so people won't step on him.
   B. Max puts Freak on his shoulders so Freak can see where Blade and his gang are.
   C. Max puts Freak on his shoulders so Freak can see the fireworks.
   D. Max puts Freak on his shoulders when Freak gets tired.

9. Describe what happens to Freak and Max after the fireworks.
   A. Tony D. and his gang chase Freak and Max, but because Freak is on Max's shoulders he can direct Max into the millpond, where they escape but get stuck in the mud.
   B. Tony D. and his gang catch Max and Freak at the millpond and throw them into the water.
   C. Max and Freak go to the soda shop because fireworks make Max thirsty, but Tony D. and his gang won't let them go in.
   D. Max and Freak are chased home by Tony D. and his gang.

10. How do Freak and Max get out of the pond after escaping from Tony D. and his gang?
    A. Freak whistles loudly to get the attention of the police. They use ropes to pull Max out.
    B. Max pulls loose from the mud and walks back to shore.
    C. The police call the fire department, and they use ladders to get Freak and Max out.
    D. Freak swims to shore, and Max walks to shore.

11. After rescuing Freak and Max from the pond muck, who does the cop say Max is?
    A. The cop says Max is a hoodlum.
    B. The cop says Max is Gram's grandson.
    C. The cop says Max is a trouble maker.
    D. The cop says he is Kenny (Killer) Kane's boy.

12. When the police officers ask for the boys' names after rescuing them, what name does Kevin give the police?
    A. Freak the Mighty
    B. Freak the Man
    C. Max the Great
    D. Mighty Max

Freak The Mighty Multiple Choice Questions Chapters 8 - 10

Chapters 8 - 10
1. How do Grim and Gram react to Max's being a hero?
    A. Grim and Gram take Max to get his favorite ice cream.
    B. Grim and Gram don't believe Max is a hero.
    C. Gram makes a fuss, and Grim calls Max "son" for the first time.
    D. Grim and Gram have a party to honor Max.

2. What does Max think about rescuing Freak?
    A. Max thinks Freak rescued him with his genius brain.
    B. Max thinks he may not be as bad as everyone thinks.
    C. Max thinks he really is a hero.
    D. Max thinks it is not big deal because he was saving himself, too.

3. What does Gram ask Max to do with regards to the hoodlum boy? What is his response?
    A. She wants Max to promise her he will keep away from him; Max tells her he will run.
    B. She wants Max to beat him up the next time he comes near Freak; Max tells Gram she is really cool.
    C. She wants Max to be friends with Tony D.; Max asks her if she has lost her mind.
    D. She wants Max to call the police if he sees Blade near the house; Max tells her he would be the laughing stock of the school if he calls the police.

4. What has become a habit for Max and Freak when they go out together?
    A. Freak picks a new quest everyday, and Max goes along.
    B. Max pulls Freak around the neighborhood in the American Flyer.
    C. Freak rides high on Max's shoulders and uses his little feet to steer Max.
    D. Freak teaches Max a new word everyday.

5. What secret does Max promise to keep about the Medical Research building?
    A. It is a secret laboratory called The Experimental Bionics Unit; Freak will enter the lab and be the first bionically improved human.
    B. It is a secret laboratory called The Experimental Brain Unit, and they study smart people like Freak.
    C. It is a secret laboratory called The Experimental Robot Unit, and they make robots to help handicapped people.
    D. It is a secret laboratory called The Experimental Disease Unit, and they are looking for a cure to Freak's disease.

6. What does Freak tell Max when he asks if the transplant will hurt and if it is dangerous?
    A. Freak says, "It will not hurt because I will be asleep. And it is not dangerous."
    B. Freak says, "Bionic parts feel no pain. The only danger is broken parts."
    C. Freak says, "Maybe just a little, but it is not at all dangerous."
    D. Freak says, "Sure it will hurt. Life is dangerous."

Freak The Mighty Multiple Choice Questions Chapters 8 - 10 page 2

7. What is the quest Freak and Max have to wait until exactly three in the morning to do?
    A. The quest is a treasure hunt.
    B. The quest is to rescue a damsel in distress.
    C. The quest is to slay a dragon.
    D. The quest is to recover King Arthur's crown.

8. What is the treasure in the storm drain?
    A. The treasure is a gold ring.
    B. The treasure is a money clip with money still attached.
    C. The treasure is a wallet.
    D. The treasure is a purse.

9. How did the treasure get into the storm drain?
    A. Freak and Max do not know how it got into the sewer.
    B. Tony D. put it there after he took the money.
    C. Loretta dropped it while she was running from Tony D. and his gang.
    D. Freak tells Max he saw one of Tony D.'s punks stuff it in.

Freak The Mighty Multiple Choice Questions Chapters 11 - 13

Chapters 11 - 13
1. What does Max call the New Tenements?
    A. He calls them the New Testaments or just the Testaments.
    B. He calls them a slum, just like Grim.
    C. He calls them the Towering Inferno because the fire department is always putting out fires.
    D. He doesn't call them anything; he is just afraid to go anywhere near them.

2. What type of people live in the Testaments?
    A. Rich people live there.
    B. Only single people live there.
    C. Poor people and dope fiends live there.
    D. Biker gangs live there.

3. Which is **not** true about Loretta Lee.
    A. The "treasure purse" Max and Freak find belong to her.
    B. She knew Killer Kane and Gwen.
    C. She lives in the New Tenements with Iggy.
    D. She is Max's aunt.

4. Why does Max like Freak riding on his shoulders?
    A. He likes Freak telling him which way to go.
    B. He likes having a really smart brain on his shoulders, helping him think.
    C. He likes Freak being able to see if Tony D. is anywhere around.
    D. He likes building up his mussels, and carrying Freak makes him strong.

5. What does Max know about Iggy?
    A. Iggy is a friend of Kevin's father.
    B. Iggy was a cook in prison and knew Killer Kane.
    C. Iggy is the boss of The Panheads, a bad-news motorcycle gang.
    D. Iggy stole the money from Loretta and put her purse in the storm drain.

6. Why does Iggy let Max and Freak leave without messing with them?
    A. He did not want Gwen to come looking for Max and Freak.
    B. He did not want any trouble with the cops.
    C. He likes Max and feels sorry for Freak.
    D. He did not want Killer Kane to know he was messing with his kid.

7. What does Freak tell Max about his father's leaving after he was born?
    A. "Good riddance to bad rubbish."
    B. "It does not matter; the Fair Gwen and I make out fine without him."
    C. "Gwen the Fair missed him for a while, but its okay now."
    D. "Gwen said it was her fault he left."

Freak The Mighty Multiple Choice Questions Chapters 11 - 13 page 2

8. Why does Gram agree to sign the papers allowing Max to be in the smart classes?
    A. Gram agrees so Max can carry Freak around to classes.
    B. Grim asks her to give it a try since nothing else has worked.
    C. Gwen talks Gram into signing the papers.
    D. Gram wants what is best for Max and the principal thinks it will help.

9. What happens in Mrs. Donelli's class that gets Max and Freak sent to the principal's office?
    A. The class makes fun of Max and Freak so Freak climbs onto Max's shoulders, rasing his fists and punching the air calling out, "Freak the Mighty! Freak the Mighty!"
    B. One of Tony D.'s gang calls Freak a goon and Max punches him.
    C. Max won't answer any questions until Freak gives him the answer.
    D. Freak and Max won't pay attention to Mrs. Donelli.

10. What does Freak teach Max that no one else has been able to do?
    A. Freak teaches Max how to look a word up in the dictionary.
    B. Freak teaches Max how to use a computer.
    C. Freak has been showing Max how to read a whole book, and it all makes sense.
    D. Freak has been showing Max how to get out of the down under.

11. How is reading different from writing to Max?
    A. Writing is a lot easier than reading.
    B. Reading is how words are just voices on paper and writing is like talking.
    C. Reading is more fun because it's like an adventure.
    D. Writing is hard because Max cannot spell.

12. Why does Max think Mrs. Addison called him to the office?
    A. Max thinks Mrs. Addison is going to find him a tutor.
    B. Max thinks Mrs. Addison is giving him detention.
    C. Max thinks Mrs. Addison is worried about him carrying Freak on his shoulders.
    D. Max thinks Mrs. Addison was going to put him back in the learning disabled class.

13. What does Mrs. Addison promise Max regarding his father?
    A. Mrs. Addison promises Max he would not have to do anything he did not want to.
    B. Mrs. Addison promises Max she will talk to Grim and Gram.
    C. Mrs. Addison promises Max he will be able to see his father.
    D. Mrs. Addison promises Max she will get his letters to his father.

14. What happens to Freak while Max is getting him more chop suey?
    A. Tony D. finds Freak alone and beats him up.
    B. Freak chokes on the chop suey.
    C. Freak gets Mrs. Addison to tell him why she called Max to the office.
    D. Tony D. dumps chop suey on Freak's head.

Freak The Mighty Multiple Choice Questions Chapters 14 - 16

Chapters 14 - 16
1. Why does Freak **not** want Gwen to hear Max talking about the robot stuff?
    A. The very idea strikes fear in her heart.
    B. She thinks Freak will die.
    C. The idea of Freak being a robot makes her sad.
    D. She thinks Freak should keep it a secret.

2. Why does Freak need a new body?
    A. Freak's legs are too small for the rest of his body.
    B. Freak's head is to large for the rest of his body.
    C. Freak is growing on the inside but not on the outside.
    D. Freak is small for his age.

3. While Max is in the down under wrapping Christmas presents he hears shouting. Why are Gram and Grim shouting?
    A. Gram wants Max to go back to the L.D. classes, but Grim doesn't agree.
    B. Grim is angry because Gram let Max stay home from school.
    C. Grim wants Gram to stop treating Max like a child.
    D. Grim wants to get a gun to protect his family, but Gram doesn't want a gun in the house.

4. What does Grim tell Max about his father?
    A. Grim tells Max his father is up for parole.
    B. Grim tells Max he will be going to live with his father.
    C. Grim tells Max he will never be allowed to see his father.
    D. Grim tells Max his father will never get out of prison.

5. On Christmas Eve what do Freak, Max, Grim, Gram, and Gwen do?
    A. They all have dinner and pretend everything is normal; no one talks about *Him*.
    B. They all have dinner together at Gram and Grim's and go to Gwen's for desert.
    C. They all have dinner together and go to church.
    D. They all have dinner and talk about Killer Kane.

6. Describe the box and gift Freak gives to Max Christmas Eve. What does Max think of his gift from Freak?
    A. The box is a pyramid, wrapped in red paper; inside is a Swiss Army knife. Max thinks it is the coolest knife he has ever seen.
    B. The box is pointed at the top like a pyramid, wrapped in Sunday comics; inside the box is a dictionary that Freak has written for Max. Max thinks the dictionary is the best of all his gifts.
    C. The box is pointed and wrapped in Santa gift paper; inside is a book about King Arthur. Max really hoped Freak would get him something other than a book.
    D. The box is almost as big as Max, wrapped in green paper; there is nothing inside the box. Max did not like Freak's joke gift at all.

Freak The Mighty Multiple Choice Questions Chapters 14 - 16 page 2

7. What happens to Max in the night on Christmas Eve?
    A. Max dreams about King Arthur and the Fair Gwen.
    B. Grim tells Max he will have to see his father when he gets out of prison.
    C. Freak comes to get him for another quest.
    D. His father sneaks in to his room.

8. What does Max's father tell him is the truth?
    A. He tells Max Iggy killed his mother, and that is the truth.
    B. He tells Max his mother is still alive, and that is the truth.
    C. He tells Max he never killed anybody, and that is the truth.
    D. He tells Max he killed his mother, and that is the truth.

9. What has Max always feared about his father?
    A. Max was afraid his father would hurt Grim and Gram.
    B. Max always feared his father would get out of jail one day.
    C. Max always feared being like his father.
    D. Max always feared his father would come for him in the night.

10. Where does Killer Kane take Max on Christmas Eve?
    A. He takes Max to Iggy and Loretta's apartment in the New Testaments.
    B. He takes Max to Freak's house; he holds Gwen, Freak, and Max hostage.
    C. He takes Max to a hide out in the Tenements.
    D. He doesn't take him anywhere; he hides in the down under.

Freak The Mighty Multiple Choice Questions Chapters 17 - 19

Chapters 17 - 19
1. Where does Iggy take Max and Killer Kane on Christmas Eve?
    A. Iggy takes them to an apartment that belongs to an old woman who has gone to visit her sister for the holidays.
    B. Iggy takes them to his biker hideout, where they will have protection.
    C. Iggy doesn't take them anywhere; Loretta takes them to an old woman's apartment.
    D. Iggy takes them to a hotel and pays for the room.

2. What does Killer Kane want Max to know?
    A. He wants Max to know he killed his mother.
    B. He wants Max to know that it was Iggy who killed his mother.
    C. He wants Max to know his mother left when he was a little boy.
    D. He wants Max to know he never killed anybody and he sent Max presents from prison.

3. What does Killer Kane swear on the Bible?
    A. He swears he has always loved Max.
    B. He swears he did not kill Max's mother.
    C. He swears he did not break out of prison.
    D. He swears if Max tries to get away he will kill him.

4. What is Killer Kane's plan for the future?
    A. He plans to join The Panheads and rob banks.
    B. He plans to move to another state with Max and make a fresh start.
    C. He plans to leave Max with his grandparents and start a new life.
    D. He plans to become a traveling minister.

5. Where does Killer Kane take Max to hide from the cops?
    A. He takes Max back to the down under because the cops have already searched there.
    B. He takes Max to The Panheads' hide out.
    C. He takes Max to a boarded-up building that used to be part of the Testaments until a fire burned it out.
    D. He takes Max to the RV they will be using for their traveling ministry.

6. Who first comes to help Max escape from his father?
    A. Loretta Lee comes to help Max.
    B. The police come to help Max.
    C. Grim comes to help Max.
    D. Iggy comes to help Max.

Freak The Mighty Multiple Choice Questions Chapters 17 - 19 page 2

7. What is the escape plan Loretta describes to Max?
    A. Loretta tells Max to sit tight, the police are there waiting for Killer Kane to come out.
    B. Loretta tells Max that Iggy will keep Killer Kane busy while she gets Max loose.
    C. Loretta tells Max that Iggy is going to knock Killer Kane out, and then it will be safe to go to the police.
    D. Loretta tells Max she will come back for him after Killer Kane goes to sleep.

8. What happens while Loretta is untying Max?
    A. Max's father catches her and ties her up next to Max.
    B. Max's father catches her and kills her with a knife.
    C. Max's father catches her and chokes her.
    D. Max's father catches her and knocks her out.

Freak The Mighty Multiple Choice Questions Chapters 20 - 22

Chapters 20 - 22
1. What does Max do to help Loretta?
    A. Max takes Killer Kane's knife and threatens him with it.
    B. Max runs out of the building calling for the police to help Loretta.
    C. Max hits his father to make him let go of Loretta's neck.
    D. Max falls on top of Killer Kane to try to shove him off of Loretta.

2. What does Max remember as he sees his father strangling Loretta?
    A. He remembers his father killing his mother.
    B. He remembers Iggy is the one who killed his mother.
    C. He remembers Grim killing his mother.
    D. He remembers his mother leaving him and his dad.

3. How does Killer Kane react to Max's memory about his mother's death?
    A. He is happy Max has finally remembered the truth.
    B. He is angry and hits Max.
    C. He tells Max he was only four years old and that he could not possibly recall that event.
    D. He tells Max, "Memory is a tricky thing not to be trusted."

4. What did Max do when he was four that cost Killer Kane years?
    A. After his father killed his mother, Max testified against his father.
    B. After his father killed his mother, Max ran to a window, broke it with his hand, and yelled for someone to come and help his mother.
    C. Max told Grim and Gram what his father had done, and they had him put in jail.
    D. Max lied to the police when they asked him who had killed his mother.

5. Why does Max's father try to strangle him?
    A. Max tries to save Loretta.
    B. Max threatens to go to the police and tell them about his mother.
    C. Killer Kane has to "clean this mess up" and get rid of Max.
    D. Max is calling for Iggy to come help save Loretta.

6. Who comes to rescue Max and Loretta from Killer Kane?
    A. Freak comes to the rescue.
    B. Grim comes to the rescue.
    C. The police come to the rescue.
    D. Iggy comes to the rescue.

7. How do Freak and Max get away from Killer Kane?
    A. Freak sprays Killer Kane with bug spray.
    B. Freak squirts Killer Kane with a mixture of soap, curry powder, and vinegar.
    C. Freak sprays Killer Kane with bleach.
    D. Freak squirts Killer Kane in the eyes with sulfuric acid.

Freak The Mighty Multiple Choice Questions Chapters 20 - 22 page 2

8. What does everyone say would happen to Killer Kane?
    A. He would be blind the rest of his life.
    B. This time he would be locked up in a high-security prison.
    C. This time they would lock him up for good.
    D. He would be out on parole in a few years.

9. What do the papers call Loretta Lee?
    A. The papers call Loretta the Heroic Biker Chick.
    B. The papers call Loretta the Heroic Babe.
    C. The papers call Loretta the Heroine Babe.
    D. The papers call Loretta the Heroic Biker Babe.

10. What does Freak tell Max Dr. Spivak says about his unique status?
    A. Dr. Spivak says Freak's unique status is questionable.
    B. Dr. Spivak says Freak's unique status makes him an object of intense curiosity.
    C. Dr. Spivak says Freak's unique status makes his DNA very valuable.
    D. Dr. Spivak says Freak's unique status makes him eligible for the transplant.

11. What is different about school after Christmas vacation?
    A. Everyone is jealous Max and Freak got their pictures in the papers, and Mrs. Donelli calls them "the dynamic duo."
    B. Everyone wants to be friends with Freak and Max now that they are heroes.
    C. Gram is still worried about Killer Kane, so she will not let Freak and Max walk home from school alone.
    D. Kevin becomes popular for saving Max's life; Max is jealous of all the attention Freak is getting.

12. What happens to Killer Kane?
    A. He is found guilty and has to serve 20 years plus his original sentence.
    B. He proves that Iggy is the one who killed Max's mother.
    C. He is found guilty and has to serve life because of the three strikes rule.
    D. He makes a deal and pleads guilty, which means he will serve out the rest of his original sentence plus ten more years.

13. Max is still upset about being like his father. What does Grim say to Max?
    A. "Even though you are the spitting image of your father, that doesn't mean you will have his personality."
    B. "All you got from him is your looks and your size. You've got your mother's heart, and that's what counts."
    C. "You may look like your father but you act like your mother."
    D. "Don't worry son; I'll keep you straight."

Freak The Mighty Multiple Choice Questions Chapters 20 - 22 page 3

14. While walking home on the last day of school what does Freak tell Max about remembering?
    A. Freak says, "Remembering is like watching a TV rerun in your head."
    B. Freak tells Max it is a good thing he remembered the truth about his mother.
    C. Freak says, "Remembering is just an invention of the mind."
    D. Freak tells Max he only has to remember the good times with his mother.

15. Why is Freak's birthday like two birthdays?
    A. Freak's birthday is like two because Freak the Mighty is almost a year old.
    B. Freak's birthday is like two because Gwen always has two parties for Freak.
    C. Freak's birthday is like two because this year Freak is popular at school.
    D. Freak's birthday is like two because Max's birthday is the same day.

16. What happens to Freak on his birthday?
    A. Freak's father shows up with a present.
    B. Freak falls from Max's shoulders and breaks his arm.
    C. Freak's new friends surprise him with a birthday party.
    D. Freak has a seizure and is taken to the hospital.

Freak The Mighty Multiple Choice Questions Chapters 23 - 25

Chapters 23 - 25
1. What does Max take to the hospital and why?
    A. Max takes Freak's dictionary because he knows Freak would want it in his room.
    B. Max takes the old ornithopter bird hoping Freak will see it flittering by his window.
    C. Max takes Freak some of Grim's cookies to cheer him up.
    D. Max takes a book about King Arthur to read to Freak.

2. Who finds Max outside the hospital, and where is he taken?
    A. Gwen finds Max and takes him to see Freak.
    B. Gwen finds Max and takes him home.
    C. Loretta finds Max and takes him to get a soda.
    D. Grim finds Max and takes him to see Freak.

3. Describe what Max sees and feels in the ICU.
    A. Max is scared at first but then he sees all the electronic gear and thinks its cool.
    B. Max sees Freak hooked up to electronic gear and tubes; he is a little worried but thinks it is all part of the transplant.
    C. Max is afraid of all the nurses and electronic machinery.
    D. Max is scared when he sees Freak and how small he looks on the bed with tubes going into his arms and up his nose.

4. What does Freak tell Max about The Bionic Unit?
    A. Freak tells Max The Bionic Unit is something he made up, and there is no operation to repair his body.
    B. Freak tells Max The Bionic Unit is on red alert, and tonight they will take him down there for his special operation.
    C. Freak tells Max The Bionic Unit is waiting for the final test results, and they will be ready to do the transplant in a few days.
    D. Freak tells Max Dr. Spivak and The Bionic Unit are ready to perform the transplant.

5. Freak gives Max a book. What does he tell Max to do with it?
    A. Freak gives Max a book with blank pages and tells Max to fill it with their adventures.
    B. Freak gives Max his dictionary and asks him to keep it in the down under.
    C. Freak gives Max a book with blank pages and tells Max to write a new King Arthur quest story.
    D. Freak gives Max a book with blank pages and tells him to write his own dictionary.

6. What happens when Freak starts coughing in the ICU?
    A. The machine next to Freak's bed starts beeping, and the nurse makes Max leave.
    B. Freak starts to choke, and Max runs for help.
    C. The doctor and nurses are swarming all over the room and Dr. Spivak tells Max to leave.
    D. The tube in Freak's nose pops out.

Freak The Mighty Multiple Choice Questions Chapters 23 - 25 page 2

7. What does Max do with the book from Freak?
   A. Max gives the book to Gwen to keep until he is ready to write in it.
   B. Max puts the book in the pyramid box for safekeeping and for good luck.
   C. Max throws the book away, knowing he will never be able to write as well as Freak.
   D. Max asks Gram to keep the book for him.

8. What does Max find out when he gets to the ICU?
   A. Freak has had his transplant.
   B. Freak is in a coma.
   C. Freak has been moved to The Bionic Unit.
   D. Freak has died.

9. What does Dr. Spivak tell Max when he says she lied to Freak about his new bionic body?
   A. She did not lie to Freak. She tried to once when he was seven, but he looked his disease up in a medical dictionary.
   B. She only lied to protect Freak from the truth.
   C. She did not lie to Freak; he made up The Bionic Unit to make Max feel better.
   D. She lied because Gwen asked her to never tell Freak he was dying.

10. How does Freak die?
    A. Freak's transplant was unsuccessful.
    B. Freak's heart was just got too big for his body.
    C. Freak's lungs were too small for his body.
    D. Freak died from an infection he contracted in The Bionic Unit.

11. What does Max do after Freak dies? How does Max feel?
    A. Max is very lonely and spends a lot of time with Gwen.
    B. Max refuses to go to school; he feels he will never be able to learn without Freak.
    C. Max hides in the down under, feeling like a balloon somebody has let all the air out of.
    D. Max is very angry Freak lied to him about the transplant, and he destroys the book Freak had given him.

12. What does Grim tell Max about living and having Freak as a friend?
    A. Grim tells Max living is not easy; he should be very grateful to have had a friend like Freak.
    B. Grim tells Max he was lucky to have a friend like Freak; now it was time to get on with living the rest of his life.
    C. Grim tells Max life is tough, and having Freak for a friend made it a little easier for a while.
    D. Grim tells Max it isn't how long you have, but what you do with the time you have. He also said that most people go through life never having a friend like Freak.

Freak The Mighty Multiple Choice Questions Chapters 23 - 25 page 3

13. How does Max feel when he goes back to school?
    A. Max finds he likes school now that everyone is being nice to him because his best friend died.
    B. Max hates every minute, especially how people kept feeling sorry for him, as if he were the one who died.
    C. Max hates every minute, especially now that he no longer has Freak for a brain.
    D. Max is not happy, but he is trying to do his best so Freak would be proud of him.

14. What does Tony D. say to Max when he returns to school? What does Max do?
    A. Tony D. tells Max it is a shame what happened to Freak. Max blows up and tells him if he ever felt sorry for him again, he'd put him headfirst in the millpond and pound him down into the mud like a fence post.
    B. Tony D. tells Max Freak got just what he deserved, and Max punches him in the face.
    C. Tony D. says hello to Max, but Max just ignores him and walks away.
    D. Tony D. tells Max how sorry he is about Freak; Max becomes one of Tony D.'s gang.

15. Who does Max see that winter after Freak dies, and what does she say to him?
    A. Max sees Gwen, and she tells him she is remarried and going to have a baby.
    B. Max sees Loretta. When she asks him what he is doing, he says, "Nothing." She gives him a long look and says, "It's time to get on with living, kid."
    C. Max sees Gwen. When she asks him what he is doing, he says, "Nothing." She gives him a long look and says, "Nothing is a drag, kid. Think about it."
    D. Max sees Loretta. When she asks him what he is doing, he says, "Nothing." She gives him a long look and says, "Nothing is a drag, kid. Think about it."

16. What does Max do with the empty book?
    A. Max writes a new King Arthur story.
    B. Max writes *Freak the Mighty*.
    C. Max writes a dictionary.
    D. Max leaves the book in the pyramid box.

ANSWER KEY - MULTIPLE CHOICE STUDY/QUIZ QUESTIONS
Freak The Mighty

	Chapters 1 - 4	Chapters 5 - 7	Chapters 8 - 10	Chapters 11 - 13	Chapters 14 - 16	Chapters 17 - 19	Chapters 20 - 22	Chapters 23 - 25
1	B	D	C	A	A	A	D	B
2	C	C	A	C	C	D	A	A
3	B	A	A	D	D	B	C	D
4	B	B	C	B	A	D	B	B
5	A	A	A	C	A	C	C	A
6	D	B	D	D	B	A	A	C
7	C	D	A	A	D	B	B	B
8	B	C	D	B	C	C	C	D
9	A	A	D	A	D		D	A
10	D	A		C	A		B	B
11	A	D		B			A	C
12	B	A		D			D	D
13	D			A			B	B
14	B			B			C	A
15	A						A	D
16	B						D	B

PREREADING VOCABULARY WORKSHEETS

VOCABULARY CHAPTERS 1 - 4 *Freak The Mighty*

Part I: Using Prior Knowledge and Contextual Clues
Below are the sentences in which the vocabulary words appear in the text. Read the sentence. Use any clues you can find in the sentence combined with your prior knowledge, and write what you think the underlined words mean on the lines provided.

1. . . . because I knew what a rotten lie that hug stuff was. Oh, I *knew*.
   That's when I got my first look at Freak, that year of the <u>phony</u> hugs.

   _____

2. Except later it was Freak himself who taught me that remembering is a great <u>invention</u> of the mind, and if you try hard enough you can remember anything, whether it really happened or not.

   _____

3. So maybe he wasn't really all *that* <u>fierce</u> in day care, except I'm pretty sure he did hit a kid with his crutch once, whacked the little brat pretty good.

   _____

4. "I said identify yourself, earthling, or suffer the <u>consequences</u>."

   _____

5. <u>Scuttle</u> into your dim hole in the ground, Maxwell dear.

   _____

6. "All mechanical objects require periodic maintenance. We'll schedule installation of a new <u>propulsion</u> unit as soon as the Fair Gwen of Air gets a replacement."

   _____

7. "Grim would be, I suppose, a <u>sobriquet</u> for your grandfather, based on his demeanor."

   _____

8. "Grim would be, I suppose, a sobriquet for your grandfather, based on his <u>demeanor</u>."

   _____

Freak the Mighty Vocabulary Chapters 1 - 4 Continued

Part II: Determining the Meaning
Match the vocabulary words to their dictionary definitions.

	Answer	Vocabulary Word	Definition
1		phony	a. the way a person behaves
2		invention	b. nickname
3		fierce	c. run hurriedly with short, quick steps
4		consequences	d. violent or aggressive; ferocious
5		scuttle	e. something newly created
6		propulsion	f. fake
7		sobriquet	g. results of ones actions
8		demeanor	h. force that sends forward

VOCABULARY CHAPTERS 5 - 7 *Freak The Mighty*

Part I: Using Prior Knowledge and Contextual Clues
Below are the sentences in which the vocabulary words appear in the text. Read the sentence. Use any clues you can find in the sentence combined with your prior knowledge, and write what you think the underlined words mean on the lines provided.

1. ". . . she said she's delighted that you and Kevin are going to be friends."

   _____

2. "She's quite a remarkable young woman, you know. Raising that poor boy all on her own."

   _____

3. "We were all of us living over in the tenements in those days, because the rent was so cheap and we were all just starting out."

   _____

4. Gwen says, "Kevin please," and her voice is real small, like she's embarrassed."

   _____

5. "Expel the object!" Freak shouts. "Regurgitate, you big moron!"

   _____

6. "Expel the object!" Freak shouts. "Regurgitate, you big moron!"

   _____

7. "Amazing perspective up here," he's saying. "This is what you see all the time."

   _____

Freak the Mighty Vocabulary Chapters 5 - 7 Continued

8. "They've locked on to us. Their <u>trajectory</u> is converging. Go to the left," he says. "Make it quick if you want to live!"

_____

9. "They've locked on to us. Their trajectory is <u>converging</u>. Go to the left," he says. "Make it quick if you want to live!"

_____

10. In a small voice I say, "Tell me what to do," and Freak pats me on the shoulder and says, "Just give me a nanosecond to process the <u>alternatives</u>."

_____

Part II: Determining the Meaning
   Match the vocabulary words to their dictionary definitions.

	Answer	Vocabulary Word	Definition
1		delighted	a. to vomit
2		remarkable	b. apartment houses over-crowded and poorly maintained
3		tenements	c. the path of a moving body or particle
4		embarrassed	d. a view or outlook
5		expel	e. choices
6		regurgitate	f. very happy
7		perspective	g. to feel self-conscious or ill at ease
8		trajectory	h. eject forcefully
9		converging	i. uncommon; worthy of notice
10		alternatives	j. coming together in one place

VOCABULARY CHAPTERS 8 - 10 *Freak The Mighty*

Part I: Using Prior Knowledge and Contextual Clues
Below are the sentences in which the vocabulary words appear in the text. Read the sentence. Use any clues you can find in the sentence combined with your prior knowledge, and write what you think the underlined words mean on the lines provided.

1. . . . and it's like I'm <u>possessed</u> or something, I've no idea where the things I'm saying are coming from, or why.

   _____

2. "Promise me you'll keep away from the <u>hoodlum</u> boy and his awful friends."

   _____

3. "He's taking <u>evasive</u> action. Avoiding a confrontation."

   _____

4. "A dragon is fear of the natural world," Freak says. " An <u>archetype</u> of the unknown."

   _____

6. "That way, mighty <u>steed</u>! Yonder lies the East!"

   _____

8. "Now swear on your heart that the data you are about to receive will be <u>divulged</u> to no one."

   _____

9. "<u>Optimum</u> darkness occurs at oh-three hundred hours."

   _____

Freak the Mighty Vocabulary Chapters 8 - 10 Continued

10. "It's black," he says. "That's what counts. The <u>camouflage</u> factor."

___

11. "Pledge to me your <u>fealty</u>."

___

12. "I devised a special <u>retrieval</u> device," Freak says.

___

Part II: Determining the Meaning
   Match the vocabulary words to their dictionary definitions.

	Answer	Vocabulary Word	Definition
1		possessed	a. made known: revealed
2		hoodlum	b. an original model
3		evasive	c. act or process of getting something back
4		archetype	d. most favorable; best
5		steed	e. controlled as if by a spirit or other force
6		divulged	f. a horse
7		optimum	g. a tough and aggressive young man
8		camouflage	h. tending or intended to avoid
9		fealty	i. protective coloring or disguise
10		retrieval	j. loyalty; faithfulness

VOCABULARY CHAPTERS 11 - 13 *Freak The Mighty*

Part I: Using Prior Knowledge and Contextual Clues
Below are the sentences in which the vocabulary words appear in the text. Read the sentence. Use any clues you can find in the sentence combined with your prior knowledge, and write what you think the underlined words mean on the lines provided.

1. . . . and why Knights are bound up with <u>oaths</u>, which is not the same thing as swearing, . . .

   _____

2. "Maybe we should reconsider this <u>particular</u> quest," Freak says.

   _____

3. "We're sorry to disturb you, but we have to go home now. It's a matter of some <u>urgency</u>."

   _____

4. "You're right, he's a <u>ringer</u> for old Killer Kane. Must be his kid, huh? Sure it is."

   _____

5. . . . and my big feet never even trip me up because I'm on <u>automatic</u>, I'm this running machine.

   _____

6. Whatever, I'm rolling on the ground like a <u>moron</u> and Freak is strutting around . . . .

   _____

7. "Max, the tests have always shown that you're not <u>dyslexic</u> or disabled, and this proves it."

   _____

Freak The Mighty Vocabulary Chapters 11 - 13 Continued

8. "It's nothing short of <u>miraculous</u>, and it almost convinces me you knew how to read at your level all along and were for some reason keeping it a secret."

_____

9. Which makes me wish all of a sudden I'd done something wrong and Mrs. Addison was just giving me <u>detention</u>.

_____

Part II: Determining the Meaning
   Match the vocabulary words to their dictionary definitions.

	Answer	Vocabulary Word	Definition
1		oath	a. working by itself with little or no direct human control
2		particular	b. stupid person
3		urgency	c. like a miracle; happening without any natural or scientific explanation
4		ringer	d. having difficulty interpreting words, letters, and symbols
5		automatic	e. solemn promise
6		moron	f. informal term for a person's double
7		dyslexic	g. specific; a certain one
8		miraculous	h. punishment of being kept in school after hours
9		detention	i. need for immediate attention or action

VOCABULARY CHAPTERS 14 - 16 *Freak The Mighty*

Part I: Using Prior Knowledge and Contextual Clues
Below are the sentences in which the vocabulary words appear in the text. Read the sentence. Use any clues you can find in the sentence combined with your prior knowledge, and write what you think the underlined words mean on the lines provided.

1. "A minor incident," he says. "Easily corrected by a biogenic <u>intervention</u>."

_____

2. . . . and everything is going real good until Christmas vacation when, if you'll excuse the <u>expression</u>, all hell breaks loose.

_____

3. "I have an <u>obligation</u>," he's saying. "A man has to protect his family."

_____

4. . . . and it's driving me nuts trying to figure out what would fit inside a <u>pyramid</u>-shaped box.

_____

5. Once on the TV this dude <u>hypnotized</u> a lobster.

_____

6. Like I'm <u>paralyzed</u> and my head is empty and all there is in the world is that big hand and this cool breath like the wind.

_____

7. He's squinting around, his eyebrows are <u>furrowed</u> shadows, and he says, ...

_____

Freak The Mighty Vocabulary Chapters 14 - 16 continued

Part II: Determining the Meaning
Match the vocabulary words to their dictionary definitions.

	Answer	Vocabulary Word	Definition
1		intervention	a. caused to be incapable of movement
2		expression	b. duty
3		obligation	c. trenched; rutted; grooved; wrinkled
4		pyramid	d. word or phrase communicating an idea
5		hypnotized	e. action taken to improve a medical disorder
6		paralyzed	f. put into a trance
7		furrowed	g. structure with a square or triangular base and sloping sides that meet in a point at the top

VOCABULARY CHAPTERS 17 - 19 *Freak The Mighty*

Part I: Using Prior Knowledge and Contextual Clues
Below are the sentences in which the vocabulary words appear in the text. Read the sentence. Use any clues you can find in the sentence combined with your prior knowledge, and write what you think the underlined words mean on the lines provided.

1. "Now, your grandparents say you're nothing but a <u>dysfunctional</u> retard, but no kin of mine is a retard, and that's a fact."

   _____

2. "On account of my appearance, and because I wasn't good enough for their <u>precious</u> daughter."

   _____

3. "It was like that, only these weren't kids, they were adults who should know better, except they're so <u>ignorant</u> and hateful they believe the worst."

   _____

4. "A great <u>injustice</u> was done to me, boy," he says.

   _____

5. "This is what they call a <u>temporary</u> situation," he says.

   _____

6. "This is just a <u>precaution</u>," he says. "Can't take any chances until you see the light."

   _____

7. At first he's surprised to see me <u>trussed</u> up, then he shrugs and doesn't look at me anymore.

   _____

8. "Something small but <u>functional</u>."

   _____

9. "The <u>accommodations</u> could be better," he says. "I'll grant you that."

   _____

Freak The Mighty Vocabulary Chapters 17 - 19 Continued

Part II: Determining the Meaning
   Match the vocabulary words to their dictionary definitions.

	Answer	Vocabulary Word	Definition
1		dysfunctional	a. living space; lodgings
2		precious	b. not lasting
3		ignorant	c. something unfair and wrong
4		injustice	d. valuable; having great value
5		temporary	e. tied up
6		precaution	f. useful; practical; working
7		trussed	g. not operating normally or properly
8		functional	h. lacking knowledge
9		accommodations	i. measure taken in advance to prevent something undesirable from happening

VOCABULARY CHAPTERS 20 - 22 *Freak The Mighty*

Part I: Using Prior Knowledge and Contextual Clues
Below are the sentences in which the vocabulary words appear in the text. Read the sentence. Use any clues you can find in the sentence combined with your prior knowledge, and write what you think the underlined words mean on the lines provided.

1. "You were wearing your brown corduroy trousers," I say, talking so fast, it makes me shake inside.

   _____

2. "Good old reliable H2SO4, an oily, colorless, corrosive liquid used in dyes, paints, explosives, and many chemical experiments."

   _____

3. . . . — Killer Kane, who is still rubbing frantic at his eyes and begging for help when they put the handcuffs on him and shoved him into the back of a police van.

   _____

4. . . . in violation of parole, in violation of a restraining order, abduction of a minor, and two counts of attempted murder . . . .

   _____

5. . . . in violation of parole, in violation of a restraining order, abduction of a minor, and two counts of attempted murder . . . .

   _____

6. "Dr. Spivak says my unique status as a marvel of genetic aberration makes me an object of intense curiosity," he says . . . .

   _____

7. "Dr. Spivak says my unique status as a marvel of genetic aberration makes me an object of intense curiosity," he says . . . .

   _____

8. The Fair Gwen goes, "I suppose this means you're going to be an obnoxious teenager."

   _____

Freak The Mighty Vocabulary Worksheet Chapters 20 - 22 Continued

9. "Talk about a <u>prodigy</u>," Freak says. "One year old and already he's on his way to ninth grade."

Part II: Determining the Meaning
  Match the vocabulary words to their dictionary definitions.

	Answer	Vocabulary Word	Definition
1		trousers	a. conducted in a hurried and chaotic way; full of fear or anxiety
2		corrosive	b. one of a kind
3		frantic	c. pants
4		violate	d. extremely unpleasant
5		abduct	e. break or fail to comply with a rule or agreement
6		unique	f. unwelcome deviation from normal
7		aberration	g. young person with exceptional abilities
8		obnoxious	h. take (someone) away illegally by force or deception
9		prodigy	i. capable of destroying slowly by chemical action

Note: "Frantic" as used in the sentence is used incorrectly; it should be "rubbing frantically at his eyes."

VOCABULARY CHAPTERS 23 - 25 *Freak The Mighty*

Part I: Using Prior Knowledge and Contextual Clues
Below are the sentences in which the vocabulary words appear in the text. Read the sentence. Use any clues you can find in the sentence combined with your prior knowledge, and write what you think the underlined words mean on the lines provided.

1. The <u>intensive</u> care unit is this place where there are so many nurses, you can't hardly turn around without bumping into one. . . .

   _____

2. Every patient gets a room alone, and there's all this electronic gear the Fair Gwen says is called "<u>telemetry</u>," which means when Freak sneezes, the nurses know about it before he can wipe his nose.

   _____

3, 4. . . . when I get closer . . . I see he's got this weird little plastic button stuck in his neck. "It's called a "<u>tracheotomy</u>," he says . . . . Standard procedure to <u>facilitate</u> breathing.

   _____

   _____

5. "I'm not coming home," he says. "Not in my present <u>manifestation</u>."

   _____

6. . . . then finally they come out and say he's okay, it was just a bad spell, that they have him <u>stabilized</u>.

   _____

7. So I went and I hated every minute of it, and I <u>especially</u> hated how people kept feeling sorry for me, as if it was me who died.

   _____

Freak the Mighty Vocabulary Chapters 23 - 25 Continued

Part II: Determining the Meaning
Match the vocabulary words to their dictionary definitions.

	Answer	Vocabulary Word	Definition
1		intensive	a. incision in the windpipe made to relieve an obstruction to breathing
2		telemetry	b. concentrated; thorough
3		tracheotomy	c. to a great degree; very much
4		facilitate	d. transmission of readings to a distant receiving set or station
5		manifestation	e. balanced; made less likely to fall
6		stabilized	f. object that shows or embodies something
7		especially	g. make easier

VOCABULARY ANSWER KEY - *Freak the Mighty*

	1-4	5-7	8-10	11-13	14-16	17-19	20-22	23-25
1	F	F	E	E	E	G	C	B
2	E	I	G	G	D	D	I	D
3	D	B	H	I	B	H	A	A
4	G	G	B	F	G	C	E	G
5	C	H	F	A	F	B	H	F
6	H	A	A	B	A	I	B	E
7	B	D	D	D	C	E	F	C
8	A	C	I	C		F	D	
9		J	J	H		A	G	
10		E	C					

DAILY LESSONS

LESSON ONE

<u>Objectives</u>
    To introduce *Freak The Mighty*
    To distribute books, study guides and other related materials
    To preview the study questions and vocabulary work for Chapters 1-4

NOTE: Prior to this class period, you need to ask students each to bring in one picture of someone who is considered a "freak." It can be from a book (like *Ripley's Believe It Or Not* or *The Guinness Book of World Records*), a magazine, the Internet, or whatever sources students have available.

<u>Activity #1</u>
Give students a few minutes to look at the pictures they brought into class. They can do this in small groups, informally at random, or by everyone passing pictures to the left until they all have their original pictures back.

<u>Activity #2</u>
Tell students to take out a piece of paper and a pencil. They are to write a Dear Diary entry from the person whose picture they have. The entry should be at least twenty sentences long and can be anything students honestly feel that their person would confide to a diary. Give students ample time to complete this assignment. Collect the assignments (with the pictures, if possible, to post together on the bulletin board after class).

<u>Activity #3</u>
Read a few of the diary entries out loud to the class. Hopefully you will find that many or most of the entries express the person's sadness at being so physically different, their wishes to be accepted and not just judged on their personal appearance, etc. Use this as a springboard for a short transition discussion to introduce the book *Freak the Mighty*.

<u>Activity #4</u>
Distribute the materials students will use in this unit. Explain in detail how students are to use these materials.

    <u>Study Guides</u> Students should read the study guide questions for each reading assignment prior to beginning the reading assignment to get a feeling for what events and ideas are important in the section they are about to read. After reading the section, students will (as a class or individually) answer the questions to review the important events and ideas from that section of the book. Students should keep the study guides as study materials for the unit test. **Preview the study questions for Chapters 1-4 together as a class.**

Vocabulary   Prior to each reading assignment, students will do vocabulary work related to the section of the book they are about to read. Following the completion of the reading of the book, there will be a vocabulary review of all the words used in the vocabulary assignments. Students should keep their vocabulary work as study materials for the unit test. **Do the vocabulary worksheet for Chapters 1-4 orally, together as a class so students see how the worksheets are to be done.**

Reading Assignment Sheet   You need to fill in the reading assignment sheet to let students know by when their reading has to be completed. You can either write the assignment sheet up on a side blackboard or bulletin board and leave it there for students to see each day, or you can "ditto" copies for each student to have. In either case, you should advise students to become very familiar with the reading assignments so they know what is expected of them.

Extra Activities Center   The Unit Resource Materials portion of this LitPlan contains suggestions for an extra library of related books and articles in your classroom as well as crossword and word search puzzles. Make an extra activities center in your room where you will keep these materials for students to use. (Bring the books and articles in from the library and keep several copies of the puzzles on hand.) Explain to students that these materials are available for students to use when they finish reading assignments or other class work early.

Nonfiction Assignment Sheet   Explain to students that they each are to read at least one non-fiction piece from the in-class library at some time during the unit. Students will fill out a Nonfiction Assignment Sheet after completing the reading to help you (the teacher) evaluate their reading experiences and to help the students think about and evaluate their own reading experiences.

Books   Each school has its own rules and regulations regarding student use of school books. Advise students of the procedures that are normal for your school. Preview the book. Look at the covers, front-matter, and index.

LESSON TWO

Objectives
  To have students practice reading orally
  To read Chapters 1-4
  To evaluate students' oral reading

Activity #1
Write the following paragraph on the board (or overhead projector so it can more easily be revealed line-by-line) if you want to do this exercise as a whole-class activity, or duplicate the paragraph and give one to each student if you want students to do this exercise independently:

> Grim comrs insidr and foe once he doesn't tell me what a eat hole I'm living in, oe how it smrlls like a lockee eoom brcause I foegot to put my socks in the hampee. He sits on the rdgr fo the brd and folds his hands togrthre. I nrvre think about how old hr is brcausr he nrvre acts old, but tonight hr's all whitr and brnt and his skin is seggy.

Have students try to read (and rewrite) the passage line-by-line as a whole class, or ask students to rewrite the whole passage as it should be written.

Use this simple exercise as an example of Max's frustration with reading and explain that Max has fairly common learning disability: the letters and symbols in words get mixed up and sometimes don't make sense.

If your class is a LD class, you might choose to take this time to share with your class that Max is an LD student, too, rather than completing this exercise with them. Ask them to pay particular attention to what Max says and how he feels about his learning disability, to see if they feel the same way–or differently.

Activity #2
Have students read Chapters 1 through 4 of *Freak The Mighty* out loud in class. You probably know the best way to get readers with your class; pick students at random, ask for volunteers, or use whatever method works best for your group. If you have not yet completed an oral reading evaluation for your students this period, this would be a good opportunity to do so. Continue oral reading in class over the next couple of days until everyone's oral reading has been evaluated. Then, students may read silently for in-class reading assignments. An oral reading evaluation from is included with this unit for your convenience.

ORAL READING EVALUATION - *Freak the Mighty*

Name _____ Class____ Date _____

SKILL	EXCELLENT	GOOD	AVERAGE	FAIR	POOR
Fluency	5	4	3	2	1
Clarity	5	4	3	2	1
Audibility	5	4	3	2	1
Pronunciation	5	4	3	2	1
_____	5	4	3	2	1
_____	5	4	3	2	1

Total _____   Grade _____

Comments:

LESSON THREE

Objectives
1. To review the main ideas and events from Chapters 1-4
2. To review the study questions and vocabulary work for Chapters 5-7
3. To read Chapters 5-7
4. To evaluate students' oral reading

Activity #1
Give students a few minutes to formulate answers for the study questions for Chapters 1-4 and then discuss the answers to the questions in detail. Write the answers on the board or overhead transparency so students can have the correct answers for study purposes.

NOTE: It is a good practice in public speaking and leadership skills for individual students to take charge of leading the discussions of the study questions. Perhaps a different student could go to the front of the class and lead the discussion each day that the study questions are discussed in this unit. Of course, you should guide the discussion when appropriate and try to fill in any gaps students may leave. The study questions could really be handled in a number of different ways, including in small groups with group reports following. Occasionally you may want to use the multiple choice questions as quizzes to check students' reading comprehension. As a short review now and then, students could pair up for the first (or last, if you have time left at the end of a class period) few minutes of class to quiz each other from the study questions. Mix up methods of reviewing the materials and checking comprehension throughout the unit so students don't get bored just answering the questions the same way each day. Variety in methods will also help address the different learning styles of your students. From now on in this unit, the directions will simply say, "Discuss the answers to the study questions in detail as previously directed." You will choose the method of preparation and discussion each day based on what best suits you and your class.

Activity #2
Give students a few minutes to preview the study questions and do the vocabulary worksheet for Chapters 5-7. Take a few minutes to discuss the correct answers to the vocabulary worksheet so students have the correct answers for study purposes. You might want to post the answers to the vocabulary matching section on one section of your board and add each chapter's answers on the day that students should have completed them. If students get in the habit of checking them first thing when they come in (maybe while you take attendance), it will save you the time of going through the answers during the class period. You may occasionally wish to spot-check students' vocabulary work prior to posting the answers–just to make sure they're doing it and not just copying the answers.

Activity #3
Read Chapters 5-7. If you have not completed the oral reading evaluations, continue with those until all students have been evaluated. When all students have been evaluated, students may read silently, in pairs or small groups, or orally as a class. Reading instructions for the remainder of the unit will simply say, Read Chapter __." You will choose how your students read (silently, orally, in pairs or groups, etc.) based on what best suits you and your class. Usually a variety of reading strategies is best to give students the opportunity to comprehend the information from a variety of ways.

LESSON FOUR

Objectives
> To review the main ideas and events from Chapters 5-7
> To introduce the class's Arthurian Legend Web Quest

Activity #1
Discuss the answers to the study questions for Chapters 5-7 as previously directed.

Activity #2
You are the queen or king of your classroom. As such, you need to knight each of your students to go on a quest on your behalf. You may do this as simply or elaborately as you choose: simply make the assignment, or (in costume with a plastic sword) formally "knight" each of your students, dubbing each The (or A) Knight of (whatever that person's assigned topic is). You could hand each a "scroll" (rolled up assignment pages for that topic, tied closed) and a "shield" (blank posterboard cut in the shape of a shield, which the Knights will have to appropriately adorn for themselves, in whatever way they feel is appropriate for their topics.) Each knight should receive a To the Knight of the Quest for (Name of the Topic) page as well as the Tasks of the Quest pages (all of which follow).

Assign each student one of the topics below. It is likely that you will have two to three students doing the same topics. Students assigned to the same topics should work together to complete the assignments.

>> Thomas Malory   Guenevere
>> (King) Arthur   Gawaine
>> Camelot   The Round Table
>> Excalibur   Launcelot
>> Lady of the Lake   Galahad
>> Mordred   Quest for the Holy Grail

Explain to students that they all have similar quests to carry out. Each person has been assigned a topic. Each person (or group) will complete the required items on their assignment sheets (Tasks of the Quest), which include researching the topic, completing a written assignment, creating and presenting a Power Point (or podcast if your students are more in sync with that technology) presentation, appropriately decorating the "shield," creating a song or poem about Freak the Mighty, and bringing a tasty dish to the feast (which will be held near the end of the unit).

Give students time to read through their assignment sheets and to begin to plan their quests. Circulate through the room to answer any individual questions that arise.

To The Knight(s) of The Quest for Thomas Malory:

Be it known by all that:

Thy duty is to find out everything thou canst about Thomas Malory. O brave and fearless Knight(s) of The Quest for Thomas Malory, have stout hearts and a firm resolve to seek out all that is known about this exceedingly famous author. Magnificently complete the challenging Tasks of the Quest, and The Golden "A" could be thine.

Thou shouldst take thy barren shield and adorn it with thy knightly colours and symbols of thine own choosing. Be it known, though, that these symbols must be found on thy quest. Acquire said symbols for thy shield as thy adventure unfolds. And, be ever prepared to defend thy chosen symbols to the ruler of thine kingdom.

As a special favour to thy Liege, thou couldst adorn thy most excellent self with garb befitting a knight when thou art in the presence of thy Liege. Some symbol, some outward sign of thy knighthood, would be most pleasing and proper to wear.

Thy Liege thanks thee for undertaking this crucial quest; for thy fruitful journey shall provide The Kingdom with vital information to unlock The Secrets Of The Arthurian Legend.

Go now, brave knight(s). Study the Tasks of the Quest. Prepare yourselves for thy long and challenging journey. Be brave; be steadfast; allow no man nor beast to distract thee from thy duties.

To The Knight(s) of The Quest for Arthur:

Be it known by all that:

Thy duty is to find out everything thou canst about the legendary Arthur. O brave and fearless Knight(s) of The Quest for Arthur, have stout hearts and a firm resolve to seek out all that is known about this exceedingly famous king. Magnificently complete the challenging Tasks of the Quest, and The Golden "A" could be thine.

Thou shouldst take thy barren shield and adorn it with thy knightly colours and symbols of thine own choosing. Be it known, though, that these symbols must be found on thy quest. Acquire said symbols for thy shield as thy adventure unfolds. And, be ever prepared to defend thy chosen symbols to the ruler of thine kingdom.

As a special favour to thy Liege, thou couldst adorn thy most excellent self with garb befitting a knight when thou art in the presence of thy Liege. Some symbol, some outward sign of thy knighthood, would be most pleasing and proper to wear.

Thy Liege thanks thee for undertaking this crucial quest; for thy fruitful journey shall provide The Kingdom with vital information to unlock The Secrets Of The Arthurian Legend.

Go now, brave knight(s). Study the Tasks of the Quest. Prepare yourselves for thy long and challenging journey. Be brave; be steadfast; allow no man nor beast to distract thee from thy duties.

To The Knight(s) of The Quest for Camelot:

Be it known by all that:

Thy duty is to find out everything thou canst about the legendary Camelot. O brave and fearless Knight(s) of The Quest for Camelot, have stout hearts and a firm resolve to seek out all that is known about this exceedingly famous place. Magnificently complete the challenging Tasks of the Quest, and The Golden "A" could be thine.

Thou shouldst take thy barren shield and adorn it with thy knightly colours and symbols of thine own choosing. Be it known, though, that these symbols must be found on thy quest. Acquire said symbols for thy shield as thy adventure unfolds. And, be ever prepared to defend thy chosen symbols to the ruler of thine kingdom.

As a special favour to thy Liege, thou couldst adorn thy most excellent self with garb befitting a knight when thou art in the presence of thy Liege. Some symbol, some outward sign of thy knighthood, would be most pleasing and proper to wear.

Thy Liege thanks thee for undertaking this crucial quest; for thy fruitful journey shall provide The Kingdom with vital information to unlock The Secrets Of The Arthurian Legend.

Go now, brave knight(s). Study the Tasks of the Quest. Prepare yourselves for thy long and challenging journey. Be brave; be steadfast; allow no man nor beast to distract thee from thy duties.

To The Knight(s) of The Quest for Excalibur:

Be it known by all that:

Thy duty is to find out everything thou canst about the mighty sword Excalibur. O brave and fearless Knight(s) of The Quest for Excalibur, have stout hearts and a firm resolve to seek out all that is known about this exceedingly famous sword. Magnificently complete the challenging Tasks of the Quest, and The Golden "A" could be thine.

Thou shouldst take thy barren shield and adorn it with thy knightly colours and symbols of thine own choosing. Be it known, though, that these symbols must be found on thy quest. Acquire said symbols for thy shield as thy adventure unfolds. And, be ever prepared to defend thy chosen symbols to the ruler of thine kingdom.

As a special favour to thy Liege, thou couldst adorn thy most excellent self with garb befitting a knight when thou art in the presence of thy Liege. Some symbol, some outward sign of thy knighthood, would be most pleasing and proper to wear.

Thy Liege thanks thee for undertaking this crucial quest; for thy fruitful journey shall provide The Kingdom with vital information to unlock The Secrets Of The Arthurian Legend.

Go now, brave knight(s). Study the Tasks of the Quest. Prepare yourselves for thy long and challenging journey. Be brave; be steadfast; allow no man nor beast to distract thee from thy duties.

To The Knight(s) of The Quest for Mordred:

Be it known by all that:

Thy duty is to find out everything thou canst about Mordred of ancient times. O brave and fearless Knight(s) of The Quest for Mordred, have stout hearts and a firm resolve to seek out all that is known about this exceedingly famous person. Magnificently complete the challenging Tasks of the Quest, and The Golden "A" could be thine.

Thou shouldst take thy barren shield and adorn it with thy knightly colours and symbols of thine own choosing. Be it known, though, that these symbols must be found on thy quest. Acquire said symbols for thy shield as thy adventure unfolds. And, be ever prepared to defend thy chosen symbols to the ruler of thine kingdom.

As a special favour to thy Liege, thou couldst adorn thy most excellent self with garb befitting a knight when thou art in the presence of thy Liege. Some symbol, some outward sign of thy knighthood, would be most pleasing and proper to wear.

Thy Liege thanks thee for undertaking this crucial quest; for thy fruitful journey shall provide The Kingdom with vital information to unlock The Secrets Of The Arthurian Legend.

Go now, brave knight(s). Study the Tasks of the Quest. Prepare yourselves for thy long and challenging journey. Be brave; be steadfast; allow no man nor beast to distract thee from thy duties.

To The Knight(s) of
The Quest for The Lady of The Lake:

Be it known by all that:

Thy duty is to find out everything thou canst about The Lady of The Lake. O brave and fearless Knight(s) of The Lady of The Lake, have stout hearts and a firm resolve to seek out all that is known about this exceedingly famous lady. Magnificently complete the challenging Tasks of the Quest, and The Golden "A" could be thine.

Thou shouldst take thy barren shield and adorn it with thy knightly colours and symbols of thine own choosing. Be it known, though, that these symbols must be found on thy quest. Acquire said symbols for thy shield as thy adventure unfolds. And, be ever prepared to defend thy chosen symbols to the ruler of thine kingdom.

As a special favour to thy Liege, thou couldst adorn thy most excellent self with garb befitting a knight when thou art in the presence of thy Liege. Some symbol, some outward sign of thy knighthood, would be most pleasing and proper to wear.

Thy Liege thanks thee for undertaking this crucial quest; for thy fruitful journey shall provide The Kingdom with vital information to unlock The Secrets Of The Arthurian Legend.

Go now, brave knight(s). Study the Tasks of the Quest. Prepare yourselves for thy long and challenging journey. Be brave; be steadfast; allow no man nor beast to distract thee from thy duties.

To The Knight(s) of The Quest for Guenevere:

Be it known by all that:

Thy duty is to find out everything thou canst about legendary Arthur's beautiful Queen Guenevere. O brave and fearless Knight(s) of The Quest for Guenevere, have stout hearts and a firm resolve to seek out all that is known about this exceedingly famous woman. Magnificently complete the challenging Tasks of the Quest, and The Golden "A" could be thine.

Thou shouldst take thy barren shield and adorn it with thy knightly colours and symbols of thine own choosing. Be it known, though, that these symbols must be found on thy quest. Acquire said symbols for thy shield as thy adventure unfolds. And, be ever prepared to defend thy chosen symbols to the ruler of thine kingdom.

As a special favour to thy Liege, thou couldst adorn thy most excellent self with garb befitting a knight when thou art in the presence of thy Liege. Some symbol, some outward sign of thy knighthood, would be most pleasing and proper to wear.

Thy Liege thanks thee for undertaking this crucial quest; for thy fruitful journey shall provide The Kingdom with vital information to unlock The Secrets Of The Arthurian Legend.

Go now, brave knight(s). Study the Tasks of the Quest. Prepare yourselves for thy long and challenging journey. Be brave; be steadfast; allow no man nor beast to distract thee from thy duties.

To The Knight(s) of The Quest for Gawaine:

Be it known by all that:

Thy duty is to find out everything thou canst about the brave knight Gawaine. O brave and fearless Knight(s) of The Quest for Gawaine, have stout hearts and a firm resolve to seek out all that is known about this exceedingly brave knight. Magnificently complete the challenging Tasks of the Quest, and The Golden "A" could be thine.

Thou shouldst take thy barren shield and adorn it with thy knightly colours and symbols of thine own choosing. Be it known, though, that these symbols must be found on thy quest. Acquire said symbols for thy shield as thy adventure unfolds. And, be ever prepared to defend thy chosen symbols to the ruler of thine kingdom.

As a special favour to thy Liege, thou couldst adorn thy most excellent self with garb befitting a knight when thou art in the presence of thy Liege. Some symbol, some outward sign of thy knighthood, would be most pleasing and proper to wear.

Thy Liege thanks thee for undertaking this crucial quest; for thy fruitful journey shall provide The Kingdom with vital information to unlock The Secrets Of The Arthurian Legend.

Go now, brave knight(s). Study the Tasks of the Quest. Prepare yourselves for thy long and challenging journey. Be brave; be steadfast; allow no man nor beast to distract thee from thy duties.

To The Knight(s) of The Quest for The Round Table:

Be it known by all that:

Thy duty is to find out everything thou canst about King Arthur's famous Round Table. O brave and fearless Knight(s) of The Quest for The Round Table, have stout hearts and a firm resolve to seek out all that is known about this exceedingly famous item. Magnificently complete the challenging Tasks of the Quest, and The Golden "A" could be thine.

Thou shouldst take thy barren shield and adorn it with thy knightly colours and symbols of thine own choosing. Be it known, though, that these symbols must be found on thy quest. Acquire said symbols for thy shield as thy adventure unfolds. And, be ever prepared to defend thy chosen symbols to the ruler of thine kingdom.

As a special favour to thy Liege, thou couldst adorn thy most excellent self with garb befitting a knight when thou art in the presence of thy Liege. Some symbol, some outward sign of thy knighthood, would be most pleasing and proper to wear.

Thy Liege thanks thee for undertaking this crucial quest; for thy fruitful journey shall provide The Kingdom with vital information to unlock The Secrets Of The Arthurian Legend.

Go now, brave knight(s). Study the Tasks of the Quest. Prepare yourselves for thy long and challenging journey. Be brave; be steadfast; allow no man nor beast to distract thee from thy duties.

To The Knight(s) of The Quest for Lancelot:

Be it known by all that:

Thy duty is to find out everything thou canst about Lancelot of ancient times. O brave and fearless Knight(s) of The Quest for Lancelot, have stout hearts and a firm resolve to seek out all that is known about this exceedingly famous knight. Magnificently complete the challenging Tasks of the Quest, and The Golden "A" could be thine.

Thou shouldst take thy barren shield and adorn it with thy knightly colours and symbols of thine own choosing. Be it known, though, that these symbols must be found on thy quest. Acquire said symbols for thy shield as thy adventure unfolds. And, be ever prepared to defend thy chosen symbols to the ruler of thine kingdom.

As a special favour to thy Liege, thou couldst adorn thy most excellent self with garb befitting a knight when thou art in the presence of thy Liege. Some symbol, some outward sign of thy knighthood, would be most pleasing and proper to wear.

Thy Liege thanks thee for undertaking this crucial quest; for thy fruitful journey shall provide The Kingdom with vital information to unlock The Secrets Of The Arthurian Legend.

Go now, brave knight(s). Study the Tasks of the Quest. Prepare yourselves for thy long and challenging journey. Be brave; be steadfast; allow no man nor beast to distract thee from thy duties.

Did you know? Lancelot is also spelled Launcelot.

To The Knight(s) of The Quest for Galahad:

Be it known by all that:

Thy duty is to find out everything thou canst about Sir Galahad. O brave and fearless Knight(s) of The Quest for Galahad, have stout hearts and a firm resolve to seek out all that is known about this exceedingly famous knight. Magnificently complete the challenging Tasks of the Quest, and The Golden "A" could be thine.

Thou shouldst take thy barren shield and adorn it with thy knightly colours and symbols of thine own choosing. Be it known, though, that these symbols must be found on thy quest. Acquire said symbols for thy shield as thy adventure unfolds. And, be ever prepared to defend thy chosen symbols to the ruler of thine kingdom.

As a special favour to thy Liege, thou couldst adorn thy most excellent self with garb befitting a knight when thou art in the presence of thy Liege. Some symbol, some outward sign of thy knighthood, would be most pleasing and proper to wear.

Thy Liege thanks thee for undertaking this crucial quest; for thy fruitful journey shall provide The Kingdom with vital information to unlock The Secrets Of The Arthurian Legend.

Go now, brave knight(s). Study the Tasks of the Quest. Prepare yourselves for thy long and challenging journey. Be brave; be steadfast; allow no man nor beast to distract thee from thy duties.

To The Knight(s) of The Quest for The Holy Grail:

Be it known by all that:

Thy duty is to find out everything thou canst about The Quest for the Holy Grail. O brave and fearless Knight(s) of The Quest for The Holy Grail, have stout hearts and a firm resolve to seek out all that is known about this exceedingly famous item. Magnificently complete the challenging Tasks of the Quest, and The Golden "A" could be thine.

Thou shouldst take thy barren shield and adorn it with thy knightly colours and symbols of thine own choosing. Be it known, though, that these symbols must be found on thy quest. Acquire said symbols for thy shield as thy adventure unfolds. And, be ever prepared to defend thy chosen symbols to the ruler of thine kingdom.

As a special favour to thy Liege, thou couldst adorn thy most excellent self with garb befitting a knight when thou art in the presence of thy Liege. Some symbol, some outward sign of thy knighthood, would be most pleasing and proper to wear.

Thy Liege thanks thee for undertaking this crucial quest; for thy fruitful journey shall provide The Kingdom with vital information to unlock The Secrets Of The Arthurian Legend.

Go now, brave knight(s). Study the Tasks of the Quest. Prepare yourselves for thy long and challenging journey. Be brave; be steadfast; allow no man nor beast to distract thee from thy duties.

Tasks of the Quest

Noble and Brave Knight(s), complete these tasks to fulfill thy duties to thy Liege:

1. Use the Net of Inter to acquire the information you seek. Start in the Land of Google. Tell the friendly Knights of Google what it is you seek. They will show you many possible paths to take to begin your quest. Be careful of trickery along the way; some paths may lead you astray. It is up to you to find the correct paths on your quest.

> A Word of Advice: Follow <u>many</u> paths to their ends. It is only by traveling <u>many</u> paths that the truth can be found. Mark down which paths you have traveled and whether you have had fruitful journeys on each. Should a path contain vital information, thou shalt secure it for thy Liege, who shall also need to know from whence it came.

2. The Land of Google shall provide you with the vital information you seek. When you acquire said information, you shall proceed to the Point of Power or, if you choose, the Pod of I. Use the magical powers you find there to transform that which you have previously acquired into a magnificent presentation for thy Liege. Thy Liege has little time for unlocking The Secrets of the Arthurian Legend, so, most noble knight(s), your magnificent presentation must play out in just one act. Thy Liege hast declared that either unduly delaying thy Liege or failing to provide vital information shall result in forfeiture of The Golden "A."

3. Dear, good knight(s), records must be kept in the kingdom—lest how would those who come after know that which has come before? I beseech you, therefore, to most earnestly put pen to parchment to create a permanent record of the vital information you have acquired. As all the kingdom's knights return from their quests, their parchments shall be collected by the Royal Minister of Records who shall assemble them into The Book of the Secrets of the Arthurian Legend. A special messenger shall ride post haste to the Land of Xerox where exceedingly small scribes shall work diligently (and amazingly quickly) to make copies of The Book so that all the Knights of the Kingdom may forever hold all the Secrets of the Arthurian Legend.

(Continueth on the next scroll.)

The Tasks of the Quest Continueth . . .

4. As Sir Thomas Malory set forth the tales of the Arthurian Legend, so, too, must you, o gentle knight(s), set your creative mind to the task of telling a tale. You, no doubt, have heard stories of Giant Freak the Mighty being whispered throughout the kingdom. Thy Liege requests a song or a bit of poetry capturing the essence of Mighty Freak. In days to come there shall be a grand feast in the kingdom, celebrating the return of the knights and the unlocking of the Secrets of the Arthurian Legend. Songs and poetry shall amuse the court and the guests of the kingdom, so, bright knight(s), let your song or the rhyme of your poem be true and pleasing to all who attend!

5. Furthermore, thy Liege hath requested the display of the most excellent shields of all the kingdom's knights. Wilst you rest and feast after your arduous journey (and have no need of it), thy shield shall show thy glory and thy bravery to all peasants who come upon it. Small and unworthy Lads and Lasses who see it shall wonder at thy glory and shall barely hope to one day, perhaps, catch a glimpse of thy shining and noble self. Therefore, my most gallant knight(s), make thy shield splendid for all to see.

6. Finally, most patient knight(s), in humble gratitude for the privilege of being granted the honor of pursuing this quest, make thy Liege a fine feast. Each of the great Knights of the Kingdom shall present to the ruler of the kingdom a tasty dish upon which all shall feast upon the unlocking of the Secrets of the Arthurian Legend.

Go now, thou brave, noble, dear, good, gentle, bright, gallant, and patient Knight(s). Prepare for the journey ahead!

WRITING ASSIGNMENT #1 - *Freak the Mighty*
Writing to Inform

PROMPT
You have gathered information about your assigned topic from the Internet. Now you are to take your information and put it into a formal essay informing your Liege of what you have found so that the Secret of the Legend of Arthur can be revealed.

PREWRITING
Gather the notes you have made during your research and review them. Make a list of "categories" of information as you review. For example, you might have *background information* as a category–or perhaps *examples*, or *current references*. There are many different kinds of categories you might have; you need to look at your information and decide what groups your information falls into. After creating the categories, begin to list pieces of information under each, organizing your notes and thoughts in a logical sequence.

DRAFTING
Take your categories and notes and begin writing your essay explaining about your topic. You should have an introductory paragraph which introduces your topic. Write one paragraph in your essay for each of the categories you compiled with your notes. Use any appropriate quotations from your sources, noting the references. Your essay should also have a concluding paragraph. Make a list of the sources you found, noting which ones you actually used in your essay.

PROMPT
When you finish the rough draft of your essay, ask a student who sits near you to read it. After reading your rough draft, he/she should tell you which parts were difficult to understand, if any, and ways in which your work could be improved. Reread your essay considering your critic's comments, and make the corrections you think are necessary.

PROOFREADING
Do a final proofreading of your essay double-checking your grammar, spelling, organization, and the clarity of your ideas.

LESSON FIVE

Objectives
- To discuss bullies, gangs, and terrorists
- To preview the study questions and vocabulary work for chapters 8-10
- To read chapters 8-10

Activity #1
Distribute the Bullies, Gangs, and Terrorists Discussion Guide or display one copy of it using the overhead projector (or copy it on to your chalk/dry-erase board). You might want to expand this activity to have students discuss the situations given in small groups or pairs before discussing them as a whole class. Another possibility would be to add a guest speaker–or a panel of guests–to discuss with your class good ways of handling the situations given and ways to cope with bullies, gangs, and terrorists in our lives. How can we positively internalize the negative events we experience?

Activity #2
Give students time to preview the study questions and do the vocabulary work for chapters 8-10. Discuss the answers to the vocabulary worksheets.

Activity #3
Give the students the remainder of the class period to read chapters 8-10. If this reading assignment is not completed prior to the end of class, it should be finished prior to the next class meeting.

LESSON SIX

Objective
- To give students a few minutes to touch base with each other in the quest groups
- To review the main events and ideas from chapters 8-10.
- To preview the study questions and vocabulary for chapters 11-13
- To read chapters 11-13

Activity #1
Give students about ten minutes to meet together in their quest groups to discuss progress on their assignments.

Activity #2
Orally discuss the answers to the study questions for chapters 8-10 as directed in the first lesson. While students have their study guides out, preview the questions for chapters 11-13.

Activity #3
Do the vocabulary worksheet for chapters 11-13 orally together in class.

Activity #4
Tell students to read chapters 11-13 prior to the next class meeting. If time remains in this class period, they may start this assignment.

DISCUSSION GUIDE
Bullies, Gangs, and Terrorists

Situation #1
There's a kid who sits behind you in class. When the teacher isn't looking, the kid stretches out his/her foot and kicks your chair. It's really annoying. You've asked the person to stop, but they keep doing it. Your teacher never sees it happen. No one who sits near you will speak up to verify that it happens. How do you deal with this situation?

Situation #2
You know a person in your school who deals drugs. He/she and some of his/her friends corner you in the bathroom one day after school and try to make you use the drugs. They say if you don't comply–or if you tell anyone–they will beat you to a bloody pulp. How do you deal with this situation?

Situation #3
A message comes to your email address from an unknown source. The message says, "Death comes to those who laugh at others. Just wait and see." A few days later there is another message from the same unknown address. It says, "Feeling scared? Good. You should." How do you deal with this situation?

Situation #4
A middle-aged, creepy-looking man follows you. You look back. He smiles. He continues to follow you. He never touches you; he never says anything to you. When you catch him looking, he just always smiles. This happens on more than one occasion. How do you deal with this situation?

Situation #5
You hear that a couple of blocks from your house, a person has been killed in a drive-by shooting. How does this make you feel?

Situation #6
Terrorists attack an airport in London. Fifty people are killed. How does this make you feel? How do you think people in London feel?

Bullies, gangs, and terrorists seem to have become a part of life. How we react to and deal with these kinds of situations can have a big impact on our lives and how we live. In each situation, we have to assess the degree of danger to ourselves, consider the options we have, and try to decide the best way of dealing with the event.

What courses of action do people have against bullies, gangs, and/or terrorists?

When is a "prank" fun–and when does it become "bullying" or "terrorism"?

Think on your own for a minute: Have you ever done anything you thought was "funny" to someone and later realized that it wasn't "funny" to that person? Have you ever been a bully? Did you apologize to the person? Why or why not?

Who are the "bullies" in *Freak the Mighty* so far? Look for others as you continue to read the story.

LESSON SEVEN

Objectives
    To review the main events and ideas from chapters 11-13
    To discuss the idea of appearance versus reality
    To preview the study questions and vocabulary work for chapters 14-15
    To read chapters 14-15

NOTE: This lesson requires some props. You will need to make several packages/items for display. Make a beautifully wrapped box with pretty paper and ribbons, but inside put something ugly, disgusting, or at least disappointing. Wrap up a small package of M&Ms (or something like that) in plain paper. Wrap a similar-looking package but inside put some less kid-desirable food (like brussel sprouts or a can of anchovies). Get an old, beat-up book that's torn, worn-out, and dirty. Inside, put a MacDonald's gift certificate for an ice-cream (or something "valuable" that can be taped, unseen, inside the book cover). The idea here is to bring several items which will illustrate that appearances can be deceiving.

Activity #1
Discuss the answers to the study guide questions for chapters 11-13 as previously directed. However, count how many "items" you have brought to class, and for the last (that number) of study questions, offer a "prize" to the students with the right answers. So if you brought 4 items to class, the student getting the correct answer to question 11 would be able to choose one prize. The student getting the correct answer to question 12 would choose one prize, and so on. Let students "open" their "prizes" as they get them.

Activity #2
When you are finished with the study questions for chapters 11-13, start a discussion with your students about their expectations of what might be in the packages based on the appearances. Work into the discussion that people make judgements all the time based on what we see. If something looks desirable, we think it IS desirable. If something looks bad, we think it IS bad. This is a kind of prejudice. When applied to *people,* we can really miss the boat, so to speak, if we don't look beyond physical appearance–as is the case in *Freak the Mighty*.

In chapter 10, Freak says, "It *looks* like a piece of junk. It may very well contain fabulous wealth." Then he directs Max to drop the line down and hook the purse. The kids at school who made fun of Freak and Max obviously didn't see the fabulous wealth inside of them; they only looked at the surface and judged both boys to be "junk." Ask students to think to themselves for a minute: Is there anyone *they* have dismissed as "junk" without really *knowing* the person? There should be no oral discussion of this issue–just keep the room quiet for a few minutes to let students contemplate the question.

Activity #3
Give students time to preview the study questions and do the vocabulary work for chapters 14-15. Discuss the answers to the vocabulary worksheets.

Activity #4
Give the students the remainder of the class period to read chapters 14-15. If this reading assignment is not completed prior to the end of class, it should be finished prior to the next class meeting.

LESSON EIGHT

Objectives
>To review the main events and ideas of chapters 14-15
>To give students time to work on their quest projects
>To preview the study questions and vocabulary for chapters 16-19
>To read chapters 16-19

Activity #1
Discuss the answers to the study questions for chapters 14-15 as previously directed.

Activity #2
Take students to the library/media center (wherever they have access to the internet or researching materials) so they can finish up their research if they haven't already. Groups may use this time to meet to discuss progress on their projects. Students may work on other parts of their quest projects if they have finished their research.

Activity #3
Tell students that prior to Lesson Ten (class after next) they should preview the study questions for chapters 16-19, do the related vocabulary worksheet, and read chapters 16-19.

LESSON NINE

Objectives
>To cause students to think about the book and their own lives
>To have students practice putting their own thoughts down on paper
>To evaluate students' writing skills

Activity
Distribute Writing Assignment #2. Discuss the directions in detail and give students ample time to complete the assignment. Make sure students know the "due date" for the assignment. A Writing Evaluation form follows the assignment, for your convenience.

Note: If students finish the writing assignment early, they could complete the assignments for chapters 16-19 (made in the last class period), work on their quest projects, or review their notes or vocabulary work.

WRITING ASSIGNMENT #2 - *Freak the Mighty*
Writing Personal Opinions

PROMPT
Freak is a pretty smart person. Not only is he "book smart," but he also has learned a lot about life in a short period of time. He makes a couple of comments in particular which are worth thinking about. In chapter 9 when Max asks him if the operation isn't dangerous, he says, **"Life is dangerous."** Later, in chapter 14 he says, **"No one stays like they are. Everybody is always changing."**

Your assignment is to choose **one** of the quotes above and use it as the main idea for your essay. You may either agree or disagree with Freak, but your essay needs to be based on one of the two quotes above.

PREWRITING
First, choose which quote you want to write about. Then, think about what that quote means to you. Is it true? What examples of the truth of the statement can you find in your life, your world? Or do you find that the statement is *not* necessarily true? Why would Freak say these things? Jot down the examples you think of and really try to think through the issue presented. You need to come to a conclusion as to whether you agree with the statement or not. When you decide on your point of view, begin organizing your thoughts. Number your notes, create an outline, do whatever helps you to present your ideas in a logical fashion.

DRAFTING
Your essay should have an introductory paragraph, introducing and stating your main point. The paragraphs in the body of your essay should each clearly state one supporting point. Three supporting points is enough, but if you have more, that's fine. Then, you should write a concluding paragraph.

PROMPT
When you finish the rough draft of your essay, ask a student who sits near you to read it. After reading your rough draft, he/she should tell you which parts were difficult to understand, if any, and ways in which your work could be improved. Reread your essay considering your critic's comments, and make the corrections you think are necessary.

PROOFREADING
Do a final proofreading of your essay double-checking your grammar, spelling, organization, and the clarity of your ideas.

WRITING EVALUATION FORM - *Freak the Mighty*

Name _____ Date _____

Grade _____

Circle One For Each Item:

Grammar:	correct	errors noted on paper
Spelling:	correct	errors noted on paper
Punctuation:	correct	errors noted on paper
Legibility:	excellent	good fair poor
_____	excellent	good fair poor
_____	excellent	good fair poor

Strengths:

Weaknesses:

Comments/Suggestions:

LESSON TEN

Objectives
- To review the main events and ideas from chapters 16-19
- To preview the study questions and vocabulary for chapters 20-22
- To read chapters 20-22

Activity #1
Discuss the answers to the study questions for chapters 16-19 as previously directed. Preview the questions for chapters 20-22 while students have their study guides out.

Activity #2
Review the correct answers for the vocabulary worksheet for chapters 16-19. Either continue with the vocabulary worksheet for chapters 20-22 orally or make the assignment for students to complete the worksheet independently.

Activity #3
Tell students they should read chapters 20-22 prior to their next class meeting. Students may begin this assignment in class if time permits.

LESSON ELEVEN

Objectives
> To review the main events and ideas from chapters 20-22
> To explore a dictionary and Freak's dictionary
> To preview the study questions and vocabulary for chapters 23-25
> To read chapters 23-25

Note: If possible, you should have a class set of student dictionaries available for Activity #1. If a class set is not possible, do the next-best thing to make the activity work.

Activity #1
Distribute dictionaries to students. The point of this activity is to explore the dictionary–to look at the pages that are often skipped over, like the pages in the very front or the very back, and to look at the word listings to show students what information is actually available in the listings. Take time to explore your dictionary with your students, looking at the "other" pages as well as exploring the information that can be found in the listing. Try to show students listings for words that show many different kinds of information. The word "back," for example, has many "extras" in our American Heritage Dictionary. After you explore the dictionary for about 10-15 minutes, keep those dictionaries handy for the next activity.

Activity #2
Tell students to take out their *Freak the Mighty* books and turn to the back. The Scholastic edition we used has "Freak's Dictionary" in the back. Read through several of the listings with your students. Ask students what is different about this dictionary as compared to the other dictionary you just perused. Look up several of Freak's words in the "real" dictionary. Compare and contrast Freak's definitions with the "real" definitions of the words.

Activity #3
Ask your students each to come up with a word and a definition that would fit in Freak's dictionary. Give students a few minutes to think, and then have students share their words and definitions orally.

Activity #4
Discuss the answers to the study questions for chapters 20-22 as previously directed. Preview the study questions for chapters 23-25 while students have their study guides out.

Activity #5
Tell students they should do the vocabulary worksheet for chapters 23-25 and read those chapters prior to the next class meeting. Students may use the remainder of this class period to work on this assignment.

LESSON TWELVE

Objectives
- To review the main events and ideas from chapters 23-25
- To show students how to work more closely with the text
- To begin to explore some of the themes in the text

Activity #1
Discuss the answers to the study questions for chapters 23-25 as previously directed.

Activity #2
Divide students into groups, one group for each of the following:
- appearances versus reality
- references to the mechanical bird
- facing issues versus ignoring issues
- religious references
- robotics
- images of or references to Max as a horse
- the pyramid
- down under
- names (and the relevance of the names)
- references to reading and/or writing

Each group should look for all references to its topic throughout the book. These are a few of the things students could hunt for; feel free to add, subtract, or substitute topics. Suggest that students divide the book up, assigning specific chapters to each group member. This will speed up the process.

After students have had time to search through the text, group members should get together to discuss their findings. Does the group's topic come up at a particular point in the action? Could it be symbolic or related to a theme? Students should spend some time talking about the possibilities of the importance of their topic(s) in the book.

When students have had ample time to discuss as a group, have each group report its findings and thoughts. Use this as a springboard for discussion about the topic. Also explain to students that by closely examining the text we can find clues as to the ideas the author wants to get across to us.

LESSONS THIRTEEN AND FOURTEEN

<u>Objectives</u>
To discuss *Freak the Mighty* on a deeper than direct-recall level
To explore some of the many ideas presented by the book

<u>Activity</u>
Choose the questions from the Extra Discussion Questions/Writing Assignments which seem most appropriate for your students. A class discussion of these questions is most effective if students have been given the opportunity to formulate answers to the questions (or ideas about the quotations) prior to the discussion. To this end, you may either have all the students formulate answers to all the questions, divide your class into groups and assign one or more questions to each group, or you could assign one question to each student in your class. The option you choose will make a difference in the amount of class time needed for this activity.

NOTE:
TELL STUDENTS THAT THEY SHOULD EACH FIND A NON-FICTION ARTICLE ABOUT ANY TOPIC RELATED TO THE BOOK *FREAK THE MIGHTY*. THEY SHOULD BRING THEIR ARTICLES TO CLASS FOR LESSON SIXTEEN.

EXTRA DISCUSSION QUESTIONS/WRITING ASSIGNMENTS
Freak the Mighty

<u>Interpretive</u>
1. From what point of view is the story told? Is that important?

2. What is the setting? Could this story have been set in a different place or time and still have had the same effect?

3. How are Gram and Grim portrayed in the book? Is there either a positive or negative spin put on their characters? Give examples.

4. Give a brief but accurate character sketch of each of the main characters in the book: Freak, Max, Gram, Grim, Gwen, Killer Kane, Iggy, and Loretta.

5. List at least three things Max says that make him seem like a "real" person.

6. How is the school system portrayed in the book? Is it portrayed in either a positive or negative way? Give examples.

7. Where is the climax of the story? Defend your answer.

8. Max's relationship with Gram and Grim changes over time. How does it change, and what events change it?

<u>Critical</u>
9. Is Max as "dumb" as everyone says he is? Defend your answer.

10. Compare and contrast Max and Kevin.

11. Why can Freak help Max read when all the specialists couldn't?

12. Iggy and Loretta appear to be stereotypical "bad guys" at first. Are they really as they appear to be at first glance?

13. Compare and contrast Iggy and Killer Kane.

14. Max thinks reading is like listening and writing is like talking. Explain what he means.

15. One main idea of the story is that friendship can overcome adversity. Explain how the friendship of Max and Kevin helped each of them overcome adversity.

16. Explain why the author uses the element of King Arthur and the knights throughout the book.

17. Explain the pyramid as a symbol in the story

18. Explain the mechanical bird as a symbol in the story.

Freak the Mighty Extra Discussion Questions page 2

Critical/Personal Response
19. Is Gwen a good mother?

20. Should Max have been passed from seventh grade to eighth?

21. Did Max belong in the higher classes with Kevin?

22. Did you start to believe Killer Kane when he kept telling Max he didn't kill his mother? How did he try to convince Max?

Personal Response
23. Did you like this book? Why or why not?

24. The description of the 4th of July holiday celebration was rather cynical. Describe the holiday of your choice at your house.

25. Do you think most people jump to conclusions about other people based on appearances, or do you think most people are open-minded and accepting of others regardless of appearance? Why?

Quotations
1. I never had a brain until Freak came along and let me borrow his for a while, and that's the truth, the whole truth. (1)

2. . . . it was Freak himself who taught me that remembering is a great invention of the mind, and if you try hard enough you can remember anything, whether it really happened or not. (1)

3. Matter of fact, I watch *tons* of tube, but I also read tons of books so I can figure out what's true and what's fake, which isn't always easy. Books are like truth serum–if you don't read, you can't figure out what's real. (4)

4. "He's not a poor boy," I say. "You should hear him talk. I think the rest of him is so small because his brain is so big." (5)

5. . . . he's not flipped out because I picked him up and put him on my shoulders like he was a little kid instead of possibly the smartest human being in the whole world. (6)

6. Me rescuing Freak. What a joke, right? Except that's how it must have looked from a distance, because they never knew it was Freak who rescued me–or his genius brain and my big dumb body. (8)

7. "He's not running away," Grim says, real impatient. "He's taking evasive action. Avoiding a confrontation. That's a very different thing, right, Max?" (8)

Freak the Mighty Extra Discussion Questions page 3

8. Pain is just a state of mind. You can think your way out of anything, even pain. (9)

9. "Life is dangerous," Freak says, and you can tell he's thought a lot about this. After a while he kicks me with his little feet and says, "Home." (9)

10. "That? That's just a piece of junk."
    "Wrong," Freak says, real fierce. "It *looks* like a piece of junk. It may very well contain fabulous wealth. Drop the line down and see if you can hook it." (10)

11. Freak is riding up top, which he almost always does now. That way he doesn't have to wear his leg brace or carry his crutches, and besides, I like how it feels to have a really smart brain on my shoulders, helping me think. (11)

12. Good riddance to bad rubbish. (12)

13. . . . sometimes I'm *more* than Kevin. (12)

14. Freak has been showing me how to read a whole book and for some reason it all makes sense, where before it was just a bunch of words I didn't care about. (13)

15. Like Freak says, reading is just a way of listening, and I could always listen, but writing is like talking, and that's a whole other ball game. (13)

16. I swear on my honor, he can't make you do anything you don't want to do. I'm going to make that *very* clear to the parole board, and to his lawyer. Very clear indeed. (13)

17. Who knows what I might do and then not remember it? (13)

18. Mrs. Addison gives me this look, and then she goes, "You're going to be okay, Maxwell Kane. I'm sure of it now." (13)

19. I'm telling tales, my dear, not lies. Lies are mean things, and tales are meant to entertain. (15)

20. *He doesn't need a suit of armor.* (16)

21. You know what I think when I see a neighborhood like this? Hamsters, is what I think. (16)

22. They hated me from the first sight. On account of my appearance, and because I wasn't good enough for their precious daughter. As if a man should be blamed for how fearsome or cruel he looks, when in fact he's truly a loving person inside. Which I am. (17)

23. I've been locked up like an animal . . . . Every single night I cried myself to sleep and that's a fact. Killer Kane, that's just an unkind nickname they hung on me. You know how kids can be mean in school, mean as animals? It was like that, only these weren't kids, they were adults who should know better, except they're so ignorant and hateful they believe the worst. (17)

Freak the Mighty Extra Discussion Questions page 4

24. You can't trust a cripple, but I guess you know that now, don't you? (18)

25. "Dumb animal," he says. "Get up now, that's just a scratch, a little blood never hurt a man." (19)

26. I saw you kill her! I saw you kill Mom! I never forgot, not ever! I know you did it! I *know*! (20)

27. "I know Kevin has been a great help to you," she says. "But you've got a brain of your own, haven't you dear?" (21)

28. All you got from him is your looks and your size. You've got your mother's heart, and that's what counts. (21)

29. . . . it's growing up that worries me. (21)

30. . . . you can't *really* get what it means to be Freak the Mighty unless you *are* Freak the Mighty. (22)

31. "I'm not coming home," he says. "Not in my present manifestation." (23)

32. That night I put the empty book in the pyramid box for safekeeping, and for good luck. (23)

33. A bunch of them jump on me and I keep going, running around in circles like an accident of nature until finally there are so many of them on me, I can't stand up anymore. (24)

34. Everybody needs something to hope for. Don't call it a lie. Kevin wasn't a liar. (24)

35. Grim tried to tell me it isn't how long you've got that matters, it's what you do with the time you have, but that sounded so lame and puny next to Freak dying that I just didn't want to hear it. (25)

36. Nothing is a drag, kid. Think about it.

LESSON FIFTEEN

Objectives
To review all of the vocabulary work done in this unit

Activity
Choose one (or more) of the vocabulary review activities listed below and spend your class period as directed in the activity. Some of the materials for these review activities are located in the Vocabulary Resource Materials section in this LitPlan.

NOTE: Remind students to bring their non-fiction articles relating to *Freak* to your next class meeting.

VOCABULARY REVIEW ACTIVITIES

1. Divide your class into two teams and have an old-fashioned spelling or definition bee.

2. Give each of your students (or students in groups of two, three or four) a *Freak the Mighty* Vocabulary Word Search Puzzle. The person (group) to find all of the vocabulary words in the puzzle first wins.

3. Give students a *Freak the Mighty* Vocabulary Word Search Puzzle without the word list. The person or group to find the most vocabulary words in the puzzle wins.

4. Use a Freak the Mighty Vocabulary Crossword Puzzle. Put the puzzle onto a transparency on the overhead projector (so everyone can see it), and do the puzzle together as a class.

5. Give students a *Freak the Mighty* Vocabulary Matching Worksheet to do.

6. Divide your class into two teams. Use *Freak the Mighty* vocabulary words with their letters jumbled as a word list. Student 1 from Team A faces off against Student 1 from Team B. You write the first jumbled word on the board. The first student (1A or 1B) to unscramble the word wins the chance for his/her team to score points. If 1A wins the jumble, go to student 2A and give him/her a definition. He/she must give you the correct spelling of the vocabulary word which fits that definition. If he/she does, Team A scores a point, and you give student 3A a definition for which you expect a correctly spelled matching vocabulary word. Continue giving Team A definitions until some team member makes an incorrect response. An incorrect response sends the game back to the jumbled-word face off, this time with students 2A and 2B. Instead of repeating giving definitions to the first few students of each team, continue with the student after the one who gave the last incorrect response on the team. For example, if Team B wins the jumbled-word face-off, and student 5B gave the last incorrect answer for Team B, you would start this round of definition questions with student 6B, and so on. The team with the most points wins!

7. Have students write a story in which they correctly use as many vocabulary words as possible. Have students read their compositions orally! Post the most original compositions on your bulletin board!

LESSON SIXTEEN

Objectives:
      To encourage students to read current non-fiction
      To tie the ideas in *Freak the Mighty* to current life
      To have students share a variety of information about topics related to the book

Activity #1
Distribute the Non-fiction Assignment Sheets. Tell students to take a few minutes to read (or re-read) the articles they have brought to class and then to fill out the Non-fiction Assignment Sheets for their articles.

Activity #2
Have students share with each other the information they learned from their articles. You may have them do this with partners (rotating partners every few minutes), as individual oral reports to the class, in small groups, or in whatever way you think will best benefit your students.

NONFICTION ASSIGNMENT SHEET - *Freak the Mighty*
(To be completed after reading the required nonfiction article)

Name _____ Date _____

Title of Nonfiction Read _____

Written By _____ Publication Date _____

I. Factual Summary: Write a short summary of the piece you read.

II. Vocabulary
    1. With which vocabulary words in the piece did you encounter some degree of difficulty?

    2. How did you resolve your lack of understanding with these words?

III. Interpretation: What was the main point the author wanted you to get from reading his work?

IV. Criticism
    1. With which points of the piece did you agree or find easy to accept? Why?

    2. With which points of the piece did you disagree or find difficult to believe? Why?

V. Personal Response: What do you think about this piece? <u>OR</u> How does this piece influence your ideas?

LESSON SEVENTEEN

<u>Objectives</u>
    To strengthen students' abilities to evaluate persuasion
    To practice persuasive writing
    To further explore the character of Killer Kane
    To evaluate students' writing skills

<u>Activity #1</u>
Review the section of the book from the time Killer Kane gets Max through his arrest. Focus on the specific passages where Killer Kane talks to Max, and isolate the techniques he uses to try to convince Max that he was actually innocent. List the techniques where students can see them.

Ask students if they believed Killer Kane before Max said that he had witnessed his mother's murder. If they did, ask why.

Explain that we are persuaded daily by friends, family, the media, and others. Likewise, we daily persuade others. Give examples.

<u>Activity #2</u>
Distribute Writing Assignment #3. Discuss the directions in detail and give students ample time to complete the assignment.

NOTE:
It would be fun to have a few students deliver their closing arguments to the class, especially if you have a few "hams" in your classroom. If you wish to take it more seriously, you could do a mini-lesson about oral delivery, require each student to actually deliver his/her closing arguments, and grade students on their deliveries.

WRITING ASSIGNMENT #3
Freak the Mighty
Writing To Persuade

PROMPT
You are the prosecuting attorney for Killer Kane's trial for the attempted murders of Max and Loretta. Write your closing arguments that you will deliver to the jury.

PREWRITING
What is Killer Kane accused of? What evidence has been given against him? What has his defense been? What would you persuade *you* to convict him and throw away the key if *you* were on the jury? Think about and jot down answers to all of these questions. Now think about how you can best convince that jury to convict. What tactics will you use? How will you start? Where will the climax of your argument be? Think about tactics you use to get what *you* want from people. Are any of those tactics helpful here? Make notes about possible tactics and delivery. Visualize it: you are standing in front of the jury. What will you say? Make an outline. Arrange your thoughts to be as persuasive as possible.

DRAFTING
Your argument might be fairly short and dramatic–or it might be long and convincing, point-by-point. Follow your outline and actually write out what you will say to the jury. Include any important body language you would use at the appropriate places (such as [pound fist on table] or [scowl and frown] or whatever you choose).

PROMPT
When you finish the rough draft of your argument, ask a student who sits near you to read it. After reading your rough draft, he/she should tell you which parts were difficult to understand, if any, and ways in which your work could be improved. Reread your essay considering your critic's comments, and make the corrections you think are necessary.

PROOFREADING
Do a final proofreading of your argument double-checking your grammar, spelling, organization, and the clarity of your ideas.

NOTE: Be prepared to orally deliver your closing arguments to your classmates!

LESSON EIGHTEEN AND NINETEEN

<u>Objectives</u>
    To conclude the Quest Projects
    To learn about the Arthurian Legend

<u>Activity</u>
Students should come to class in costume if you have suggested that. They should bring their tasty dishes and put them on a table you have pre-set for the occasion. Give students a few minutes to socialize, then begin the Power Point or iPod presentations about each of the assigned topics. Students should display their shields during their reports, then ceremoniously hang them in the place(s) you have designated. You could dress as the King or Queen, and the reports could be addressed directly to you. Invite students to share their poems and songs about Freak the Mighty in between presentations.

You could assign half of the groups to report in Lesson Eighteen and half to report in Lesson Nineteen. In that case only half would have to dress, bring tasty dishes, and report each day.

Have fun with this! Grade whatever portions you wish and/or maybe have prizes for Best Costume, Best Report, Best Shield, Most Courteous Knight, or whatever. Have a photographer from your yearbook staff or a student in your class be the official photographer of the event!

As a follow up or as extra credit, have students write articles for your school newspaper about your class's Quest for the Arthurian Legend–or informative articles about the legend itself!

You could also have the class members all contribute to a class scrapbook of the event.

Students could compile their presentations into one huge presentation about the Arthurian Legend, which could be copied and stored in your resource room for other classes to use.

LESSON TWENTY

Objective
    To review the main ideas and events in *Freak The Mighty*

Activity
    Choose one of the review games/activities suggested in this unit and spend your class time as directed there.

REVIEW GAMES/ACTIVITIES *Freak The Mighty*

1. Ask the class to make up a unit test for *Freak The Mighty*. The test should have 4 sections: matching, true/false, short answer, and essay. Students may use 1/2 period to make the test and then swap papers and use the other 1/2 class period to take a test a classmate has devised. (open book) You may want to use the unit test included in this packet or take questions from the students' unit tests to formulate your own test.

2. Take 1/2 period for students to make up true and false questions (including the answers). Collect the papers and divide the class into two teams. Draw a big tic-tac-toe board on the chalk board. Make one team X and one team O. Ask questions to each side, giving each student one turn. If the question is answered correctly, that students' team's letter (X or O) is placed in the box. If the answer is incorrect, no letter is placed in the box. The object is to get three in a row like tic-tac-toe. You may want to keep track of the number of games won for each team.

3. Take 1/2 period for students to make up questions (true/false and short answer). Collect the questions. Divide the class into two teams. You'll alternate asking questions to individual members of teams A & B (like in a spelling bee). The question keeps going from A to B until it is correctly answered, then a new question is asked. A correct answer does not allow the team to get another question. Correct answers are +2 points; incorrect answers are -1 point.

4. Have students pair up and quiz each other from their study guides and class notes.

5. Give students an *Freak The Mighty* crossword puzzle to complete.

6. Divide your class into two teams. Use *Freak The Mighty* crossword words with their letters jumbled as a word list. Student 1 from Team A faces off against Student 1 from Team B. You write the first jumbled word on the board. The first student (1A or 1B) to unscramble the word wins the chance for his/her team to score points. If 1A wins the jumble, go to student 2A and give him/her a clue. He/she must give you the correct word which matches that clue. If he/she does, Team A scores a point, and you give student 3A a clue for which you expect another correct response. Continue giving Team A clues until some team member makes an incorrect response. An incorrect response sends the game back to the jumbled-word face off, this time with students 2A and 2B. Instead of repeating giving clues to the first few students of each team, continue with the student after the one who gave the last incorrect response on the team. For example, if Team B wins the the jumbled-word face-off, and student 5B gave the last incorrect answer for Team B, you would start this round of clue questions with student 6B, and so on. The team with the most points wins!

Review Games Page 2

8. Play What's My Line?. This is similar to the old television show. Students assume the roles of different characters from the epic. One student gives clues to the class, or to a panel of contestants. The contestants try to guess the identity of the guest. Students may enjoy assisting you in creating rules and procedures for the game.

9. Play Jeopardy. Divide the class into two groups. Assign each group a category or book from the epic and have them devise answers for that category. Play the game according to the television show procedures.

10. Play Drawing in the Details. This is similar to Pictionary. Divide students into teams. A student from one team draws a scene from the epic. (You may want to specify the Book or section.) Drawings should be kept simple, to keep the pace lively. Students in the opposing team locate the scene in their books and read it aloud. If they are incorrect, the illustrator's team has a chance to guess. Involve students in setting up a scoring system and any other necessary rules.

UNIT TESTS

SHORT ANSWER UNIT TEST 1 *Freak the Mighty*

I. Matching/Identification

____ 1. HERO

____ 2. GWEN

____ 3. LORETTA

____ 4. EXCALIBUR

____ 5. MILLPOND

____ 6. DICTIONARY

____ 7. GUINEVERE

____ 8. BIONIC

____ 9. GRIM

____ 10. PHILBRICK

____ 11. SEIZURE

____ 12. FREAK

____ 13. MAX

____ 14. WHISTLES

____ 15. ICU

____ 16. INSIDE

____ 17. DONELLI

____ 18. PURSE

____ 19. IGGY

____ 20. CRETIN

____ 21. FLOATING

____ 22. TESTAMENTS

____ 23. ARTHUR

____ 24. GRAM

____ 25. BOOK

A. How Max feels when he goes to the place in his head

B. Loretta and Iggy live in the New _____

C. Max's grandmother

D. Where Freak the Mighty is born

E. What the police call Max for saving Kevin

F. Boss of the Panheads

G. How Freak gets the cops attention

H. King ___, once a wimpy little kid, an orphan who pulled a sword from the stone

I. Author of Freak the Mighty

J. The Experimental ____ Unit: where Freak will become the first bionically improved human

K. Freak gives Max a blank one and tells him to fill it with their adventures.

L. Freak grew on the ____ but not on the outside

M. The Mighty part of Freak the Mighty

N. Heroic Biker Babe

O. One of the names Kevin uses for his mother

P. Where Freak dies

Q. Freak writes one for Max

R. What Freak calls Tony D

S. What happens to Freak on his birthday

T. Friend of Max's mother

U. King Arthur's magical sword

V. He talks like a dictionary and sits on Max's shoulders

W. The object of the treasure hunt

X. He built the Down Under.

Y. Sends Max and Freak to the principals office

Freak the Mighty Short Answer Unit Test 1 Page 2

II. Short Answer

1. Who is telling the story?

2. What is Grim's concern about Maxwell?

3. What observation does Max make about how Freak talks?

4. What happens to Max and Freak when they are walking to the millpond to see the fireworks?

5. Why does Gram agree to sign the papers allowing Max to be in the smart classes?

6. What happens to Max in the night on Christmas Eve?

7. What does Max's father tell him is the truth?

8. Who comes to rescue Max and Loretta from Killer Kane?

9. What happens to Killer Kane?

10. Describe what Max sees and feels in the ICU.

11. How did Freak die?

12. What does Max do with the empty book?

Freak the Mighty Short Answer Unit Test 1 Page 3

III. Quotations: Identify the importance of 5 of the following quotes in the book.

1. Matter of fact, I watch *tons* of tube, but I also read tons of books so I can figure out what's true and what's fake, which isn't always easy. Books are like truth serum–if you don't read, you can't figure out what's real.

2. Me rescuing Freak. What a joke, right? Except that's how it must have looked from a distance, because they never knew it was Freak who rescued me–or his genius brain and my big dumb body.

3. "Life is dangerous," Freak says, and you can tell he's thought a lot about this. After a while he kicks me with his little feet and says, "Home."

4. Freak is riding up top, which he almost always does now. That way he doesn't have to wear his leg brace or carry his crutches, and besides, I like how it feels to have a really smart brain on my shoulders, helping me think.

5. Like Freak says, reading is just a way of listening, and I could always listen, but writing is like talking, and that's a whole other ball game.

6. Grim tried to tell me it isn't how long you've got that matters, it's what yo do with the time you have, but that sounded so lame and puny next to Freak dying that I just didn't want to hear it.

7. Nothing is a drag, kid. Think about it.

Freak the Mighty Short Answer Unit Test 1 Page 4

IV. Vocabulary

Write the vocabulary words you are given. After writing them down, go back and write in their definitions.

Word	Definition
1	
2	
3	
4	
5	
6	
7	
8	
9	
10	

ANSWER KEY SHORT ANSWER UNIT TEST 1 *Freak the Mighty*

I. Matching/Identification

E	1. HERO	A.	How Max feels when he goes to the place in his head
T	2. GWEN	B.	Loretta and Iggy live in the New _____
N	3. LORETTA	C.	Max's grandmother
U	4. EXCALIBUR	D.	Where Freak the Mighty is born
D	5. MILLPOND	E.	What the police call Max for saving Kevin
Q	6. DICTIONARY	F.	Boss of the Panheads
O	7. GUINEVERE	G.	How Freak gets the cops attention
J	8. BIONIC	H.	King ___, once a wimpy little kid, an orphan who pulled a sword from the stone
X	9. GRIM	I.	Author of Freak the Mighty
I	10. PHILBRICK	J.	The Experimental _____ Unit: where Freak will become the first bionically improved human
S	11. SEIZURE	K.	Freak gives Max a blank one and tells him to fill it with their adventures.
V	12. FREAK	L.	Freak grew on the _____ but not on the outside
M	13. MAX	M.	The Mighty part of Freak the Mighty
G	14. WHISTLES	N.	Heroic Biker Babe
P	15. ICU	O.	One of the names Kevin uses for his mother
L	16. INSIDE	P.	Where Freak dies
Y	17. DONELLI	Q.	Freak writes one for Max
W	18. PURSE	R.	What Freak calls Tony D
F	19. IGGY	S.	What happens to Freak on his birthday
R	20. CRETIN	T.	Friend of Max's mother
A	21. FLOATING	U.	King Arthur's magical sword
B	22. TESTAMENTS	V.	He talks like a dictionary and sits on Max's shoulders
H	23. ARTHUR	W.	The object of the treasure hunt
C	24. GRAM	X.	He built the Down Under.
K	25. BOOK	Y.	Sends Max and Freak to the principals office

Freak the Mighty Short Answer Unit Test 1 Answer Key Page 2

II. Short Answer
1. Who is telling the story?
    Maxwell is the narrator of the story.
2. What is Grim's concern about Maxwell?
    He is concerned because Maxwell looks like his father and is afraid Max will inherit his father's character.
3. What observation does Max make about how Freak talks?
    Max says Freak talks ". . . like right out of a dictionary. So smart you can hardly believe it."
4. What happens to Max and Freak when they are walking to the mill pond to see the fireworks?
    Tony D. and his gang stop them and harass them. They are "saved" when the gang members run away when a police car drives nearby.
5. Why does Gram agree to sign the papers allowing Max to be in the smart classes?
    Grim asks her to give it a try since nothing else has worked. He thinks that maybe Max just needs a friend.
6. What happens to Max in the night on Christmas Eve?
    His father sneaks into his room and tells Max, "I came back like I promised." Killer Kane clamps his hand over Max's mouth. Max feels paralyzed and his head is empty and all there is in the world is a big hand and cool breath like the wind.
7. What does Max's father tell him is the truth?
    He says he never killed anybody, and that is the truth.
8. Who comes to rescue Max and Loretta from Killer Kane?
    Freak comes to the rescue.
9. What happens to Killer Kane?
    Just before the trial starts, Killer Kane pleads guilty. He makes a deal to serve out the rest of his original sentence plus ten more years.
10. Describe what Max sees and feels in the ICU.
    There are so many nurses he can't hardly turn around without bumping in to one. There is all this electronic gear Gwen says is called telemetry. Max is not scared until he sees Freak and how small he looks on the bed with tubes going into his arms and up his nose.
11. How did Freak die?
    Dr. Spivak tells Max that Freak's heart just got too big for his body.
12. What does Max do with the empty book?
    Max writes *Freak the Mighty*.

III. Quotations:
    Answers to the quotations will vary depending on your class discussions and the level of your students.

Freak the Mighty Short Answer Unit Test 1 Answer Key Page 3

IV. Vocabulary
   Write the vocabulary words you have chosen to test.

Word	Definition
1	
2	
3	
4	
5	
6	
7	
8	
9	
10	

SHORT ANSWER UNIT TEST 2 *Freak the Mighty*

I. Matching/Identification

____ 1. TESTAMENTS   A. Loretta and Iggy live in the New _____

____ 2. BOOK   B. One of the names Kevin uses for his mother

____ 3. GWEN   C. What happens to Freak on his birthday

____ 4. READ   D. Friend of Max's mother

____ 5. HIM   E. How Max feels when he goes to the place in his head

____ 6. WHISTLES   F. Killer____: Max's father

____ 7. WRITING   G. He talks like a dictionary and sits on Max's shoulders

____ 8. PAIN   H. According to Freak, it is just a state of mind.

____ 9. GUILTY   I. Where Freak dies

____10. SHOULDERS   J. How Freak gets the cops attention

____11. FREAK   K. Killer Kane violated his

____12. ICU   L. King Arthur's magical sword

____13. PAROLE   M. Freak taught Max how to do this better

____14. SPIVAK   N. Killer Kane planned to become one to get money

____15. SEIZURE   O. Freak gives Max a blank one and tells him to fill it with their adventures.

____16. PHILBRICK   P. The object of the treasure hunt

____17. DONELLI   Q. Sends Max and Freak to the principals office

____18. KANE   R. Killer Kane's method of killing

____19. GUINEVERE   S. _____ is just an invention of the mind.

____20. FLOATING   T. It is like talking, according to Max

____21. PURSE   U. Author of Freak the Mighty

____22. EXCALIBUR   V. Max's father

____23. PREACHER   W. Freak sits on Max's

____24. REMEMBERING   X. Kevin's doctor

____25. STRANGLE   Y. Killer Kane's plea before going to trial

Freak the Mighty Short Answer Unit Test 2 Page 2

II. Short Answer
1. Max sees Freak for the first time in day care. What does Max think of Freak?

2. What didn't Max have until Freak moved down the street?

3. Why is Freak really interested in the knights?

4. People say that Max is the "spitting image" of his father. Why is it bad for Max to look like his father?

5. Describe what happens to Freak and Max after the fireworks.

6. How do Grim and Gram react to Max's being a hero?

7. What has become a habit for Max and Freak when they go out together?

8. What does Freak teach Max that no one else has been able to do?

9. Why does Freak need a new body?

10. What has Max always feared about his father?

11 What does Max remember as he sees his father strangling Loretta?

12. What does Max do after Freak dies? How does Max feel?

Freak the Mighty Short Answer Unit Test 2 Page 3

III. Quotations: Identify the importance of 5 of the following quotes in the book.

1. . . . it was Freak himself who taught me that remembering is a great invention of the mind, and if you try hard enough you can remember anything, whether it really happened or not.

2. "He's not running away," Grim says, real impatient. "He's taking evasive action. Avoiding a confrontation. That's a very different thing, right, Max?"

3. I swear on my honor, he can't make you do anything you don't want to do. I'm going to make that *very* clear to the parole board, and to his lawyer. Very clear indeed.

4. They hated me from the first sight. On account of my appearance, and because I wasn't good enough for their precious daughter. As if a man should be blamed for how fearsome or cruel he looks, when in fact he's truly a loving person inside. Which I am.

5. "I know Kevin has been a great help to you," she says. "But you've got a brain of your own, haven't you dear?"

6. All you got from him is your looks and your size. You've got your mother's heart, and that's what counts.

7. Nothing is a drag, kid. Think about it.

Freak the Mighty Short Answer Unit Test 2 Page 4

IV. Vocabulary

Write the vocabulary words you are given. After writing them down, go back and write in their definitions.

Word	Definition
1	
2	
3	
4	
5	
6	
7	
8	
9	
10	

ANSWER KEY SHORT ANSWER UNIT TEST 2 *Freak the Mighty*

I. Matching/Identification

A	1. TESTAMENTS	A. Loretta and Iggy live in the New _____
O	2. BOOK	B. One of the names Kevin uses for his mother
D	3. GWEN	C. What happens to Freak on his birthday
M	4. READ	D. Friend of Max's mother
V	5. HIM	E. How Max feels when he goes to the place in his head
J	6. WHISTLES	F. Killer____: Max's father
T	7. WRITING	G. He talks like a dictionary and sits on Max's shoulders
H	8. PAIN	H. According to Freak, it is just a state of mind.
Y	9. GUILTY	I. Where Freak dies
W	10. SHOULDERS	J. How Freak gets the cops attention
G	11. FREAK	K. Killer Kane violated his
I	12. ICU	L. King Arthur's magical sword
K	13. PAROLE	M. Freak taught Max how to do this better
X	14. SPIVAK	N. Killer Kane planned to become one to get money
C	15. SEIZURE	O. Freak gives Max a blank one and tells him to fill it with their adventures.
U	16. PHILBRICK	P. The object of the treasure hunt
Q	17. DONELLI	Q. Sends Max and Freak to the principals office
F	18. KANE	R. Killer Kane's method of killing
B	19. GUINEVERE	S. _____ is just an invention of the mind.
E	20. FLOATING	T. It is like talking, according to Max
P	21. PURSE	U. Author of Freak the Mighty
L	22. EXCALIBUR	V. Max's father
N	23. PREACHER	W. Freak sits on Max's
S	24. REMEMBERING	X. Kevin's doctor
R	25. STRANGLE	Y. Killer Kane's plea before going to trial

Freak the Mighty Short Answer Unit Test 2 Answer Key Page 2

II. Short Answer
1. Max sees Freak for the first time in day care. What does Max think of Freak?
    He thinks Freak is fierce, but he thinks Freak's crutches are cool and the leg braces are even more cool.
2. What didn't Max have until Freak moved down the street?
    Max did not have a brain until Freak moved down the street.
3. Why is Freak really interested in the knights?
    He believes the knights were like the first human version of robots. Hundreds of years before they had computers they were already attempting to exceed the design limitations of the human body.
4. People say that Max is the "spitting image" of his father. Why is it bad for Max to look like his father?
    Everyone in town knows his father is in prison and why.
5. Describe what happens to Freak and Max after the fireworks.
    Tony D. and his gang again come after Freak and Max. Because he is up high, Freak can see who is coming after them and where they are. He directs Max, who is running with Freak on his shoulders, by kicking him on the right or left. Freak directs Max into the millpond, where they escape but get stuck in the mud.
6. How do Grim and Gram react to Max's being a hero?
    Gram makes a fuss over him, and when Max asks if he could have sugar for his coffee, Grim says, "Of course you can, son." Max has proved himself to be a "good guy," so Grim finally accepts him.
7. What has become a habit for Max and Freak when they go out together?
    Freak rides up high on Max's shoulders and uses his little feet to steer Max if he forgets where they are going.
8. What does Freak teach Max that no one else has been able to do?
    Freak has been showing Max how to read a whole book, and it all makes sense.
9. Why does Freak need a new body?
    Freak is growing on the inside but not on the outside.
10. What has Max always feared about his father?
    Max always knew his father would come for him in the night. Then he would wake up to find him there, filling the room, and that would make him feel empty.
11 What does Max remember as he sees his father strangling Loretta?
    He remembers seeing his father killing his mother.
12. What does Max do after Freak dies? How does Max feel?
    Max hides in the down under, which is why he misses the funeral and the Fair Gwen's going away. Max feels like a balloon and somebody has let all the air out. He doesn't care if the air comes back because it doesn't matter if you are going to die in the end.

III. Quotations:
    Answers to the quotations will vary depending on your class discussions and the level of your students.

Freak the Mighty Short Answer Unit Test 2 Answer Key Page 3

IV. Vocabulary

Write the vocabulary words you have chosen to test.

Word	Definition
1	
2	
3	
4	
5	
6	
7	
8	
9	
10	

ADVANCED SHORT ANSWER UNIT TEST *Freak the Mighty*

I. Matching/Identification

____ 1. TESTAMENTS   A. Loretta and Iggy live in the New _____

____ 2. BOOK   B. One of the names Kevin uses for his mother

____ 3. GWEN   C. What happens to Freak on his birthday

____ 4. READ   D. Friend of Max's mother

____ 5. HIM   E. How Max feels when he goes to the place in his head

____ 6. WHISTLES   F. Killer____: Max's father

____ 7. WRITING   G. He talks like a dictionary and sits on Max's shoulders

____ 8. PAIN   H. According to Freak, it is just a state of mind.

____ 9. GUILTY   I. Where Freak dies

____ 10. SHOULDERS   J. How Freak gets the cops attention

____ 11. FREAK   K. Killer Kane violated his

____ 12. ICU   L. King Arthur's magical sword

____ 13. PAROLE   M. Freak taught Max how to do this better

____ 14. SPIVAK   N. Killer Kane planned to become one to get money

____ 15. SEIZURE   O. Freak gives Max a blank one and tells him to fill it with their adventures.

____ 16. PHILBRICK   P. The object of the treasure hunt

____ 17. DONELLI   Q. Sends Max and Freak to the principals office

____ 18. KANE   R. Killer Kane's method of killing

____ 19. GUINEVERE   S. _____ is just an invention of the mind.

____ 20. FLOATING   T. It is like talking, according to Max

____ 21. PURSE   U. Author of Freak the Mighty

____ 22. EXCALIBUR   V. Max's father

____ 23. PREACHER   W. Freak sits on Max's

____ 24. REMEMBERING   X. Kevin's doctor

____ 25. STRANGLE   Y. Killer Kane's plea before going to trial

Freak the Mighty Advanced Short Answer Unit Test Page 2

II. Short Answer

1. Give a brief but accurate character sketch of 3 of the main characters in the book: Freak, Max, Gram, Grim, Gwen, Killer Kane, Iggy, or Loretta.

2. Where is the climax of the story? Defend your answer.

3. Max thinks reading is like listening and writing is like talking. Explain what he means.

4. Explain why the author uses the element of King Arthur and the knights throughout the book.

5. Did you start to believe Killer Kane when he kept telling Max he didn't kill his mother? How did he try to convince Max?

Freak the Mighty Advanced Short Answer Unit Test Page 3

III. Composition

Do you think most people jump to conclusions about other people based on appearances, or do you think most people are open-minded and accepting of others regardless of appearance? Why? Write a complete essay and support your ideas with examples from the book.

Freak the Mighty Advanced Short Answer Unit Test Page 4

IV. Vocabulary

Write down the vocabulary words given, then write a paragraph or two about *Freak the Mighty* correctly using 10 of the words.

MULTIPLE CHOICE UNIT TEST 1 *Freak the Mighty*

I. Matching

____ 1. EXCALIBUR A. According to Freak, it is just a state of mind.

____ 2. FREAK B. One of the names Kevin uses for his mother

____ 3. GUINEVERE C. Freak sprays Killer Kane in the eyes with fake _____ acid.

____ 4. ORNITHOPTER D. What the police call Max for saving Kevin

____ 5. IGGY E. He talks like a dictionary and sits on Max's shoulders

____ 6. REMEMBERING F. Kevin's doctor

____ 7. TESTAMENTS G. Killer Kane violated his

____ 8. HERO H. Loretta and Iggy live in the New _____

____ 9. BRAIN I. _____ is just an invention of the mind.

____ 10. GWEN J. King Arthur's magical sword

____ 11. STRANGLE K. Friend of Max's mother

____ 12. PAROLE L. He built the Down Under.

____ 13. DICTIONARY M. Killer Kane's method of killing

____ 14. BIONIC N. What Max didn't have until Freak came along.

____ 15. GRIM O. Plastic bird

____ 16. INSIDE P. Freak gives Max a blank one and tells him to fill it with their adventures.

____ 17. SULFURIC Q. Boss of the Panheads

____ 18. SPIVAK R. Max's father

____ 19. BOOK S. Author of Freak the Mighty

____ 20. PAIN T. Tony D's nickname

____ 21. PHILBRICK U. Freak writes one for Max

____ 22. MAX V. Where Freak the Mighty is born

____ 23. BLADE W. The Experimental _____ Unit: where Freak will become the first bionically improved human

____ 24. MILLPOND X. Freak grew on the _____ but not on the outside

____ 25. HIM Y. The Mighty part of Freak the Mighty

Freak the Mighty Multiple Choice Unit Test 1 page 2

II. Multiple Choice

1. Who is telling the story?
    A. Kevin is the narrator of the story.
    B. Maxwell is the narrator of the story.
    C. Gwen is the narrator of the story.
    D. Killer Kane is the narrator of the story.

2. Why is Grim concerned about Maxwell?
    A. Grim is concerned because Maxwell looks like his father and is afraid Max will inherit his father's character.
    B. Grim is concerned because Maxwell cannot read.
    C. Grim is concerned because Maxwell spends too much time in the basement.
    D. Grim is concerned because Maxwell has no friends.

3. What observation does Max make about how Freak talks?
    A. Freak talks like a robot.
    B. Freak talks like he is King Author.
    C. Freak talks like he is better than Max.
    D. Freak talks like right out of a dictionary.

4. What happens to Max and Freak when they are walking to the millpond to see the fireworks?
    A. They get lost and miss the fireworks.
    B. They are stopped and harassed by Tony D. and his gang.
    C. Max falls down and lands on Freak, hurting his leg.
    D. They find money on the street and stop to buy candy.

5. Why does Gram agree to sign the papers allowing Max to be in the smart classes?
    A. Gram agrees so Max can carry Freak around to classes.
    B. Grim asks her to give it a try since nothing else has work.
    C. Gwen talks Gram into signing the papers.
    D. Gram wants what is best for Max and the principal thinks it will help.

6. What happens to Max in the night on Christmas Eve?
    A. Max dreams about King Arthur and the Fair Gwen.
    B. Grim tells Max he will have to see his father when he gets out of prison.
    C. Freak comes to get him for another quest.
    D. His father sneaks in to his room and tells Max, "I came back like I promised."

7. What does Max's father tell him is the truth?
    A. He tells Max Iggy killed his mother, and that is the truth.
    B. He tells Max his mother is still alive, and that is the truth.
    C. He tells Max he never killed anybody, and that is the truth.
    D. He tells Max he killed his mother, and that is the truth.

Freak the Mighty Multiple Choice Unit Test 1 page 3

8. Who comes to rescue Max and Loretta from Killer Kane?
   A. Freak comes to the rescue.
   B. Grim comes to the rescue.
   C. The police come to the rescue.
   D. Iggy comes to the rescue.

9. What happens to Killer Kane?
   A. He is found guilty and has to serve 20 years plus his original sentence.
   B. He proves that Iggy is the one who killed Max's mother.
   C. He is found guilty and has to serve life because of the three strikes rule.
   D. He makes a deal and pleads guilty, which means he will serve out the rest of his original sentence plus ten more years.

10. Describe what Max sees and feels in the ICU.
    A. Max is scared at first but then he sees all the electronic gear and thinks its cool.
    B. Max sees Freak hooked up to electronic gear and tubes; he is a little worried but thinks it is all part of the transplant.
    C. Max is afraid of all the nurses and electronic machinery.
    D. Max is scared when he sees Freak and how small he looks on the bed with tubes going into his arms and up his nose.

11. How did Freak die?
    A. Freak's transplant was unsuccessful.
    B. Freak's heart just got too big for his body.
    C. Freak's lungs were too small for his body.
    D. Freak dies from an infection he contracted in The Bionic Unit.

12. What does Max do with the empty book?
    A. Max writes a new King Arthur story.
    B. Max writes *Freak the Mighty*.
    C. Max writes a dictionary.
    D. Max leaves the book in the pyramid box.

Freak the Mighty Multiple Choice Unit Test 1 page 4

III. Quotations: Match the first part of the quotation with the last part.

First Part

1. Pain is just a state of mind.

2. You know what I think when I see a neighborhood like this?

3. You can't trust a cripple,

4. I know Kevin has been a great help to you.

5. I'm not coming home,

6. Everybody need something to hope for.

7. Nothing is a drag, kid.

8. All you got from him is your looks and your size.

Second Part

A. Don't call it a lie. Kevin wasn't a liar.

B. You can think your way out of anything, even pain.

C. But I guess you know that now, don't you.

D. Hamster, is what I think.

E. Not in my present manifestation.

F. You've got your mother's heart, and that's what counts.

G. But you've got a brain of your own, haven't you dear.

H. Think about it.

Freak the Mighty Multiple Choice Unit Test 1 page 5

IV. Vocabulary

____ 1. PERSPECTIVE A. Incision in the windpipe made to relieve an obstruction to breathing
____ 2. SCUTTLE B. Something unfair and wrong
____ 3. PRODIGY C. Capable of destroying slowly by chemical action
____ 4. AUTOMATIC D. Working by itself with little or no direct human control
____ 5. DIVULGED E. Need for immediate attention or action
____ 6. PARTICULAR F. Conducted in a hurried and chaotic way; full of fear or anxiety
____ 7. FRANTIC G. A view or outlook
____ 8. TRACHEOTOMY H. One of a kind
____ 9. PARALYZED I. Duty
____ 10. CORROSIVE J. Tied up
____ 11. ABDUCT K. Tough and aggressive young man
____ 12. INJUSTICE L. Made known; revealed
____ 13. URGENCY M. To a great degree; very much
____ 14. CONSEQUENCES N. Caused to be incapable of movement
____ 15. INVENTION O. Pants
____ 16. ALTERNATIVES P. Take (someone) away illegally by force or deception
____ 17. ESPECIALLY Q. Choices
____ 18. TRUSSED R. Specific; a certain one
____ 19. MORON S. Results of one's actions
____ 20. UNIQUE T. Young person with exceptional abilities
____ 21. DEMEANOR U. Force that sends forward
____ 22. HOODLUM V. Run hurriedly with short, quick steps
____ 23. PROPULSION W. The way a person behaves
____ 24. TROUSERS X. Something newly created
____ 25. OBLIGATION Y. Stupid person

V. Essay

What do you think is the most important lesson the author wanted us to learn from reading *Freak the Mighty*? Explain your answer in detail using examples from the book.

MULTIPLE CHOICE UNIT TEST 2 *Freak the Mighty*

I. Matching

____ 1. WRITING   A. Author of Freak the Mighty

____ 2. PHILBRICK   B. Freak sprays Killer Kane in the eyes with fake _____ acid.

____ 3. EXCALIBUR   C. Max's grandmother

____ 4. KANE   D. Freak writes one for Max

____ 5. GRAM   E. Heroic Biker Babe

____ 6. PAIN   F. He talks like a dictionary and sits on Max's shoulders

____ 7. MAX   G. One of the names Kevin uses for his mother

____ 8. GUINEVERE   H. King Arthur's magical sword

____ 9. DICTIONARY   I. How Freak gets the cops attention

____ 10. BOOK   J. What happens to Freak on his birthday

____ 11. ADDISON   K. Principal

____ 12. SULFURIC   L. Where Freak dies

____ 13. HERO   M. How Max feels when he goes to the place in his head

____ 14. FREAK   N. According to Freak, it is just a state of mind.

____ 15. CRETIN   O. Boss of the Panheads

____ 16. FLOUR   P. What the police call Max for saving Kevin

____ 17. MILLPOND   Q. Sends Max and Freak to the principals office

____ 18. INSIDE   R. Freak gives Max a blank one and tells him to fill it with their adventures.

____ 19. ICU   S. It is like talking, according to Max

____ 20. DONELLI   T. Freak grew on the ____ but not on the outside

____ 21. SEIZURE   U. Killer____: Max's father

____ 22. LORETTA   V. The Mighty part of Freak the Mighty

____ 23. FLOATING   W. Where Freak the Mighty is born

____ 24. IGGY   X. What Freak calls Tony D

____ 25. WHISTLES   Y. Max at first only knows King Arthur as the brand of ____ Gram uses.

Freak the Mighty Multiple Choice Unit Test 2 page 2

II. Matching

1. Max sees Freak for the first time in day care. What does Max think of Freak?
    A. Max thinks Freak is a sad little kid.
    B. Max thinks Freak is fierce; he thinks his crutches and leg braces are cool.
    C. Max thinks Freak is bossy.
    D. Max thinks Freak is trying to impress the other kids.

2. What didn't Max have until Freak moved down the street?
    A. Max did not have a complaint.
    B. Max did not have a reading coach.
    C. Max did not have an American Flyer wagon.
    D. Max did not have a brain.

3. Why is Freak really interested in the knights?
    A. He believes the knights were the bravest men who ever lived.
    B. He believes the knights were like the first human version of robots.
    C. He wants to start a club, Freak's Knights of the Round Table.
    D. He thinks everyone should be loyal like the knights.

4. People say that Max is the "spitting image" of his father. Why is it bad for Max to look like his father?
    A. His father is scary-looking.
    B. Everyone in town knows his father is in prison and why he is there.
    C. People always stare at him.
    D. His father's picture is on a "wanted" poster.

5. Describe what happens to Freak and Max after the fireworks.
    A. Tony D. and his gang chase Freak and Max, but because Freak is on Max's shoulders he can direct Max into the mill pond, where they escape but get stuck in the mud.
    B. Tony D. and his gang catch Max and Freak at the mill pond and throw them into the water.
    C. Max and Freak go to the soda shop because fireworks make Max thirsty, but Tony D. and his gang won't let them go in.
    D. Max and Freak are chased home by Tony D. and his gang.

6. How do Grim and Gram react to Max's being a hero?
    A. Grim and Gram take Max to get his favorite ice cream.
    B. Grim and Gram don't believe Max is a hero.
    C. Gram makes a fuss and Grim calls Max "son" for the first time.
    D. Grim and Gram have a party to honor Max.

Freak the Mighty Multiple Choice Unit Test 2 page 3

7. What has become a habit for Max and Freak when they go out together?
    A. Freak picks a new quest everyday, and Max goes along.
    B. Max pulls Freak around the neighborhood in the American Flyer.
    C. Freak rides high on Max's shoulders and uses his little feet to steer Max.
    D. Freak teaches Max a new word everyday.

8. What does Freak teach Max that no one else has been able to do?
    A. Freak teaches Max how to look a word up in the dictionary.
    B. Freak teaches Max how to use a computer.
    C. Freak has been showing Max how to read a whole book, and it all makes sense.
    D. Freak has been showing Max how to get out of the down under.

9. Why does Freak need a new body?
    A. Freak's legs are too small for the rest of his body.
    B. Freak's head is to large for the rest of his body.
    C. Freak is growing on the inside but not on the outside.
    D. Freak is small for his age.

10. What has Max always feared about his father?
    A. Max was afraid his father would hurt Grim and Gram.
    B. Max always feared his father would get out of jail one day.
    C. Max always feared being like his father.
    D. Max always feared his father would come for him in the night.

11. What does Max remember as he sees his father strangling Loretta?
    A. He remembers his father killing his mother.
    B. He remembers Iggy is the one who killed his mother.
    C. He remembers Grim killing his mother.
    D. He remembers his mother leaving him and his dad.

12. What does Max do after Freak dies? How does Max feel?
    A. Max is very lonely and spends a lot of time with Gwen.
    B. Max refuses to go to school; he feels he will never be able to learn without Freak.
    C. Max hides in the down under, feeling like a balloon somebody has let all the air out of.
    D. Max is very angry Freak lied to him about the transplant, and he destroys the book Freak had given him.

Freak the Mighty Multiple Choice Unit Test 2 page 4

III. Quotations: Match the speaker to the quote.

    A. Kevin   B. Max   C. Grim   D. Gram

    E. Gwen   F. Killer Kane   G. Mrs. Addison   H. Loretta Lee

1. Good riddance to bad rubbish.

2. I swear on my honor, he can't make you do anything you don't want to do. I'm going to make that *very* clear to the parole board, and to his lawyer. Very clear indeed.

3. I'm telling tales, my dear, not lies. Lies are mean things, and tales are meant to entertain.

4. You can't trust a cripple, but I guess you know that now, don't you?

5. I saw you kill her!

6. But you've got a brain of your own, haven't you dear?

7. All you got from him is your looks and your size.

8. I'm not coming home. Not in my present manifestation.

9. Nothing is a drag, kid. Think about it.

Freak the Mighty Multiple Choice Unit Test 2 page 5

IV. Vocabulary

____ 1. REGURGITATE   A. Balanced; made less likely to fall

____ 2. TROUSERS   B. Extremely unpleasant

____ 3. REMARKABLE   C. Eject forcefully

____ 4. DETENTION   D. Uncommon; worthy of notice

____ 5. RETRIEVAL   E. Punishment of being kept in school after hours

____ 6. POSSESSED   F. Working by itself with little or no direct human control

____ 7. TRUSSED   G. To feel self-conscious or ill at ease

____ 8. STABILIZED   H. Like a miracle; happening without any natural or scientific explanation

____ 9. TENEMENTS   I. Pants

____10. DEMEANOR   J. Protective coloring or disguise

____11. PRODIGY   K. Most favorable; best

____12. OPTIMUM   L. Apartment houses over-crowed and poorly maintained

____13. AUTOMATIC   M. Controlled as if by a spirit or other force

____14. EMBARRASSED   N. Put into a trance

____15. FACILITATE   O. Something unfair and wrong

____16. CAMOUFLAGE   P. Not operating normally or properly

____17. PERSPECTIVE   Q. Act or process of getting something back

____18. FUNCTIONAL   R. A view or outlook

____19. INJUSTICE   S. Transmission of readings to a distant receiving set or station

____20. MIRACULOUS   T. To vomit

____21. EXPEL   U. Tied up

____22. DYSFUNCTIONAL   V. Useful; practical; working

____23. OBNOXIOUS   W. The way a person behaves

____24. TELEMETRY   X. Young person with exceptional abilities

____25. HYPNOTIZED   Y. Make easier

Freak the Mighty Multiple Choice Unit Test 2 page 6

V. Essay

Discuss the characters of Gram and Grim in the book as they contributed to the author's theme development. Use specific examples from the book to support your statements.

MULTIPLE CHOICE UNIT TEST ANSWER SHEET
Freak the Mighty

	Matching	Multiple Choice	Quotations	Vocabulary
1				
2				
3				
4				
5				
6				
7				
8				
9				
10				
11				
12				
13				
14				
15				
16				
17				
18				
19				
20				
21				
22				
23				
24				
25				

MULTIPLE CHOICE UNIT TEST 1 ANSWER KEY
Freak the Mighty

	Matching	Multiple Choice	Quotations	Vocabulary
1	J	B	B	G
2	E	A	D	V
3	B	D	C	T
4	O	B	G	D
5	Q	B	E	L
6	I	D	A	R
7	H	C	H	F
8	D	A	F	A
9	N	D		N
10	K	D		C
11	M	B		P
12	G	B		B
13	U			E
14	W			S
15	L			X
16	X			Q
17	C			M
18	F			J
19	P			Y
20	A			H
21	S			W
22	Y			K
23	T			U
24	V			O
25	R			I

MULTIPLE CHOICE UNIT TEST 2 ANSWER KEY
Freak the Mighty

	Matching	Multiple Choice	Quotations	Vocabulary
1	S	B	A	T
2	A	D	G	I
3	H	B	C	D
4	U	B	F	E
5	C	A	B	Q
6	N	C	D	M
7	V	C	C	U
8	G	C	A	A
9	D	C	H	L
10	R	D		W
11	K	A		X
12	B	C		K
13	P			F
14	F			G
15	X			Y
16	Y			J
17	W			R
18	T			V
19	L			O
20	Q			H
21	J			C
22	E			P
23	M			B
24	O			S
25	I			N

UNIT RESOURCE MATERIALS

BULLETIN BOARD IDEAS - *Freak the Mighty*

1. Save one corner of the board for the best of students' *Freak the Mighty* writing assignments.

2. Take one of the word search puzzles from the extra activities packet and with a marker copy it over in a large size on the bulletin board. Write the clue words to find to one side. Invite students prior to and after class to find the words and circle them on the bulletin board.

3. Write several of the most significant quotations from the book onto the board on brightly colored paper.

4. Make a bulletin board listing the vocabulary words for this unit. As you complete sections of the novel and discuss the vocabulary for each section, write the definitions on the bulletin board. (If your board is one students face frequently, it will help them learn the words.)

5. Post pictures and diary entries from the introductory lesson.

6. Decorate bulletin board to resemble the inside of a castle to help students prepare for the Quest Project. Hang the "shields" on the castle wall.

7. Create a class dictionary, post the words and definitions your students created in lesson eleven. Encourage your students to add to the list.

8. Make your bulletin board look like a castle wall, and have students put their shields on it!

EXTRA ACTIVITIES - *Freak the Mighty*

One of the difficulties in teaching a novel is that all students don't read at the same speed. One student who likes to read may take the book home and finish it in a day or two. Sometimes a few students finish the in-class assignments early. The problem, then, is finding suitable extra activities for students.

One thing that seems to help is to keep a little library in the classroom. For this unit on *Freak the Mighty*, you might check out from the school library other books by Rodman Philbrick. Any stories or articles about King Arthur, robots, medical advances regarding replacement limbs, careers in medical research or law enforcement, learning disabilities, intervention hotlines, terrorism, dealing with bullies, fireworks, police reports, etc. would also be of interest.

Other things you may keep on hand are puzzles. We have made some relating directly to *Freak the Mighty* for you. Feel free to duplicate them for your students to use.

Some students may like to draw. You might devise a contest or allow some extra-credit grade for students who draw characters or scenes from *Freak the Mighty*. Note, too, that if the students do not want to keep their drawings you may pick up some extra bulletin board materials this way. If you have a contest and you supply the prize (a CD or something like that perhaps), you could, possibly, make the drawing itself a non-returnable entry fee.

The pages which follow contain games, puzzles and worksheets. The keys, when appropriate, immediately follow the puzzle or worksheet. There are two main groups of activities: one group for the unit; that is, generally relating to *Freak the Mighty* text, and another group of activities related strictly to *Freak the Mighty* vocabulary.

Directions for these games, puzzles and worksheets are self-explanatory. The object here is to provide you with extra materials you may use in any way you choose.

MORE ACTIVITIES - *Freak the Mighty*

1. Have students work together to make a time line chronology of the events in the story. Take a large piece of construction paper and on one wall (or however you can physically arrange it in your room) and make the events of the story along it. Students may want to add drawings or cut-out pictures to represent the events (as well as a written statement).

2. Have students design a book cover (front and back and inside flaps) for *Freak the Mighty*.

3. Have students design a bulletin board (ready to be put up; not just sketched) for *Freak the Mighty*.

4. Have students write additional quest stories for Max and Kevin.

5. Rodman Philbrick has written a one-act and two-act play for the book, it is available on line free of charge. Have your students perform the play for extra credit.

6. Have students write their own personal dictionaries.

7. Have students draw a picture of their view of the first human robot.

8. Investigate bikers and biker groups. Have students learn about the history of bikes and motorcycle "gangs." How have biker groups changed over the years? What are some of the biggest gatherings now? Have the demographics of motorcycle riders changed over the years?

9. Go on a field trip to a medical research unit, a hospital, and/or an ICU.

10. Have a doctor who deals with rare medical conditions come speak to your class.

11. Ask a few local businesses to sponsor a fireworks display at your school one evening.

12. Invite a psychologist to come and discuss ways of dealing with traumatic experiences.

Freak the Mighty **Word List**

ADDISON	Principal
ARTHUR	King ___, once a wimpy little kid, an orphan who pulled a sword from the stone
BIONIC	The Experimental ____ Unit: where Freak will become the first bionically improved human
BLADE	Tony D's nickname
BOOK	Freak gives Max a blank one and tells him to fill it with their adventures.
BRAIN	What Max didn't have until Freak came along.
CHARACTER	Grim is concerned Max will inherit this from his father
COMICS	Kevin wrapped Max's Christmas present with this
CRETIN	What Freak calls Tony D
DICTIONARY	Freak writes one for Max
DONELLI	Sends Max and Freak to the principals office
EXCALIBUR	King Arthur's magical sword
FLOATING	How Max feels when he goes to the place in his head
FLOUR	Max at first only knows King Arthur as the brand of ____ Gram uses.
FREAK	He talks like a dictionary and sits on Max's shoulders
GRAM	Max's grandmother
GRIM	He built the Down Under.
GUILTY	Killer Kane's plea before going to trial
GUINEVERE	One of the names Kevin uses for his mother
GWEN	Friend of Max's mother
HERO	What the police call Max for saving Kevin
HIM	Max's father
ICU	Where Freak dies
IGGY	Boss of the Panheads
INSIDE	Freak grew on the ____ but not on the outside
KANE	Killer____: Max's father
KNIGHTS	First human version of robots, according to Freak
LIFE	____ is dangerous.
LORETTA	Heroic Biker Babe
MAX	The Mighty part of Freak the Mighty
MILLPOND	Where Freak the Mighty is born
ORNITHOPTER	Plastic bird
PAIN	According to Freak, it is just a state of mind.
PAROLE	Killer Kane violated his
PHILBRICK	Author of Freak the Mighty
PREACHER	Killer Kane planned to become one to get money
PURSE	The object of the treasure hunt
PYRAMID	Max's Christmas present from Freak is in a box shaped like a _____.
READ	Freak taught Max how to do this better
REMEMBERING	____ is just an invention of the mind.
SEIZURE	What happens to Freak on his birthday
SHOULDERS	Freak sits on Max's
SPIVAK	Kevin's doctor
STRANGLE	Killer Kane's method of killing

Freak the Mighty Word List continued

SULFURIC	Freak sprays Killer Kane in the eyes with fake _____ acid.
TESTAMENTS	Loretta and Iggy live in the New _____
WHISTLES	How Freak gets the cops attention
WRITING	It is like talking, according to Max

WORD SEARCH - Freak the Mighty

```
F C H A R A C T E R E T X K A L Z A H S L
R L N S H G S P Z A C X A K Y R T K T Z V
E D F R L J T Y R K D V C G S T T N M B F
A S U L F U R I C E I D T A E B E H D Y L
K F O K H L A C G P A W I R L M D I U M V
G C R X R M N F S D X C O S A I M H C R M
C M N W L G G M Y W G L H T O A B Z S H J
C D I Y Q T L S R V S Y S E R N N U B J M
K C T S F H E G H N P E D Y R Y T J R Y N
Q F H K L B S K R O T D P P N R N B B Q J
V W O Q O X R E W Z U P O Q N K X Y T K J
W P P N A R P T I J X L H N N Z N Y C D R
M N T Q T Y V M H Z K H D C E R N C D H D
I B E Q I K A H V Z U P D E E L S D I S F
G N R S N R A Q V S W R A M R D L F C N H
G Y E L G U I N E V E R E D I S N I T M R
Y R F M R C H W E T D M R G Q W M W I I N
K H I W S R R C L L B G I W Q O P H O L N
X R L M H E R O O E I U C E C K A I N L R
R X A X D T N W R S O I U N O N I S A P D
S X D A M I T I A R N L Y O I M N T R O Z
R T L R Z N N Y P U I T B A B F Y L Y N J
J B K N I G H T S P C Y R U O L F E N D P
W R I T I N G P H I L B R I C K L S K S H
```

ADDISON	FLOATING	INSIDE	PURSE
ARTHUR	FLOUR	KANE	PYRAMID
BIONIC	FREAK	KNIGHTS	READ
BLADE	GRAM	LIFE	REMEMBERING
BOOK	GRIM	LORETTA	SEIZURE
BRAIN	GUILTY	MAX	SHOULDERS
CHARACTER	GUINEVERE	MILLPOND	SPIVAK
COMICS	GWEN	ORNITHOPTER	STRANGLE
CRETIN	HERO	PAIN	SULFURIC
DICTIONARY	HIM	PAROLE	TESTAMENTS
DONELLI	ICU	PHILBRICK	WHISTLES
EXCALIBUR	IGGY	PREACHER	WRITING

WORD SEARCH ANSWER KEY - Freak the Mighty

```
F  C  H  A  R  A  C  T  E  R  E        E        K     A        A        S
R                    S  P     A     X        A        R  T     T
E                    T     R     D  V  C           T  T     N
A  S  U  L  F  U  R  I  C  E  I  D     A  E        E  H     D
K     O              A        P  A     I  R  L     M  I     U
      R              N        S        C  O  S  A  I  M        R
      N              G              L  H  T  O  A  B
      I              L  S           S  E  R        N        U
      T        F        E  H        E  Y  R                 R
      H        L        S        O  T  D  P
      O        O           E        U     O
      P        A              I  L     N
      T        T        M  Z        D     E           D
I     E        I  K  A        U     D  E  L           I     S
G     R        N  R  A              R  M  R           C
G     E        G  U  I  N  E  V  E  R  E  D  I  S  N  T     M
Y  R  F        C        E           M  R  G        M  W     I
   I           R        L        B  G  I  W     O  P  H     L
   L  M  H  E  R  O  O  E  I  U     C  E  C  K  A  I  N     L
      A        D     T     R  S  O     I  U  N  O  N  I  S  A  P
   X  A        I        I  A  R  N     L        O  I     N  R  O
      L        N        N  P  U  I  T     B  A              L  Y  N  D
      B  K  N  I  G  H  T  S     P     C  Y  R  U  O  L  F  E        D
W  R  I  T  I  N  G  P  H  I  L  B  R  I  C  K              S
```

ADDISON	FLOATING	INSIDE	PURSE
ARTHUR	FLOUR	KANE	PYRAMID
BIONIC	FREAK	KNIGHTS	READ
BLADE	GRAM	LIFE	REMEMBERING
BOOK	GRIM	LORETTA	SEIZURE
BRAIN	GUILTY	MAX	SHOULDERS
CHARACTER	GUINEVERE	MILLPOND	SPIVAK
COMICS	GWEN	ORNITHOPTER	STRANGLE
CRETIN	HERO	PAIN	SULFURIC
DICTIONARY	HIM	PAROLE	TESTAMENTS
DONELLI	ICU	PHILBRICK	WHISTLES
EXCALIBUR	IGGY	PREACHER	WRITING

CROSSWORD - Freak the Mighty

Across

3. Freak gives Max a blank one and tells him to fill it with their adventures.
4. Heroic Biker Babe
7. King ___, once a wimpy little kid, an orphan who pulled a sword from the stone
8. Friend of Max's mother
9. Freak grew on the ____ but not on the outside
12. The Mighty part of Freak the Mighty
13. Boss of the Panheads
15. The object of the treasure hunt
17. He talks like a dictionary and sits on Max's shoulders
18. The Experimental ____ Unit: where Freak will become the first bionically improved human
19. What the police call Max for saving Kevin
20. Principal
21. He built the Down Under.
22. King Arthur's magical sword

Down

1. Killer ____: Max's father
2. Killer Kane's method of killing
3. What Max didn't have until Freak came along.
4. ____ is dangerous.
5. Freak taught Max how to do this better
6. Loretta and Iggy live in the New _____
8. Max's grandmother
10. Kevin's doctor
11. Sends Max and Freak to the principals office
13. Where Freak dies
14. What Freak calls Tony D
15. According to Freak, it is just a state of mind.
16. What happens to Freak on his birthday
17. Max at first only knows King Arthur as the brand of ____ Gram uses.
18. Tony D's nickname
19. Max's father

CROSSWORD ANSWER KEY - Freak the Mighty

		1 K		2 S		3 B	O	O	K		4 L	5 O	R	E	6 T	T	A
			7 A	R	T	H	U	R			I		E		E		S
8 G	W	E	N		R			A			F		A		S		
R			E		A		9 I	10 N	S	11 I	D	E		D		12 M	A	X
A					N		N		P		O					M	
M		13 I	G	G	Y				I		N						
		C		L			14 C	V		E		15 P	U	R	S	E
	16 S	U		E			R	A		L		A			N	
	E				17 F	R	E	A	K		L		I			T	
	I				L		T			18 B	I	O	N	I	C	S
	Z		19 H	E	R	O		I		L						
	U		I		U			N		20 A	D	D	I	S	O	N
21 G	R	I	M		R					D						
	E									22 E	X	C	A	L	I	B	U	R

Across
3. Freak gives Max a blank one and tells him to fill it with their adventures.
4. Heroic Biker Babe
7. King ___, once a wimpy little kid, an orphan who pulled a sword from the stone
8. Friend of Max's mother
9. Freak grew on the ___ but not on the outside
12. The Mighty part of Freak the Mighty
13. Boss of the Panheads
15. The object of the treasure hunt
17. He talks like a dictionary and sits on Max's shoulders
18. The Experimental ___ Unit: where Freak will become the first bionically improved human
19. What the police call Max for saving Kevin
20. Principal
21. He built the Down Under.
22. King Arthur's magical sword

Down
1. Killer____: Max's father
2. Killer Kane's method of killing
3. What Max didn't have until Freak came along.
4. ___ is dangerous.
5. Freak taught Max how to do this better
6. Loretta and Iggy live in the New ___
8. Max's grandmother
10. Kevin's doctor
11. Sends Max and Freak to the principals office
13. Where Freak dies
14. What Freak calls Tony D
15. According to Freak, it is just a state of mind.
16. What happens to Freak on his birthday
17. Max at first only knows King Arthur as the brand of ___ Gram uses.
18. Tony D's nickname
19. Max's father

MATCHING 1 - Freak the Mighty

____ 1. SPIVAK   A. What the police call Max for saving Kevin
____ 2. CHARACTER   B. He built the Down Under.
____ 3. FLOATING   C. The object of the treasure hunt
____ 4. WRITING   D. One of the names Kevin uses for his mother
____ 5. HERO   E. Sends Max and Freak to the principals office
____ 6. GRAM   F. Grim is concerned Max will inherit this from his father
____ 7. PYRAMID   G. Where Freak dies
____ 8. DONELLI   H. Max's grandmother
____ 9. IGGY   I. Killer Kane's method of killing
____ 10. STRANGLE   J. It is like talking, according to Max
____ 11. TESTAMENTS   K. Boss of the Panheads
____ 12. DICTIONARY   L. According to Freak, it is just a state of mind.
____ 13. PAIN   M. Freak writes one for Max
____ 14. GRIM   N. How Max feels when he goes to the place in his head
____ 15. FREAK   O. Plastic bird
____ 16. GUINEVERE   P. The Mighty part of Freak the Mighty
____ 17. GUILTY   Q. What Freak calls Tony D
____ 18. MAX   R. Max's Christmas present from Freak is in a box shaped like a _____.
____ 19. ORNITHOPTER   S. He talks like a dictionary and sits on Max's shoulders
____ 20. SHOULDERS   T. Killer Kane's plea before going to trial
____ 21. PURSE   U. Kevin's doctor
____ 22. LORETTA   V. What Max didn't have until Freak came along.
____ 23. CRETIN   W. Heroic Biker Babe
____ 24. BRAIN   X. Loretta and Iggy live in the New _____
____ 25. ICU   Y. Freak sits on Max's

MATCHING 1 ANSWER KEY - Freak the Mighty

U	1. SPIVAK	A.	What the police call Max for saving Kevin
F	2. CHARACTER	B.	He built the Down Under.
N	3. FLOATING	C.	The object of the treasure hunt
J	4. WRITING	D.	One of the names Kevin uses for his mother
A	5. HERO	E.	Sends Max and Freak to the principals office
H	6. GRAM	F.	Grim is concerned Max will inherit this from his father
R	7. PYRAMID	G.	Where Freak dies
E	8. DONELLI	H.	Max's grandmother
K	9. IGGY	I.	Killer Kane's method of killing
I	10. STRANGLE	J.	It is like talking, according to Max
X	11. TESTAMENTS	K.	Boss of the Panheads
M	12. DICTIONARY	L.	According to Freak, it is just a state of mind.
L	13. PAIN	M.	Freak writes one for Max
B	14. GRIM	N.	How Max feels when he goes to the place in his head
S	15. FREAK	O.	Plastic bird
D	16. GUINEVERE	P.	The Mighty part of Freak the Mighty
T	17. GUILTY	Q.	What Freak calls Tony D
P	18. MAX	R.	Max's Christmas present from Freak is in a box shaped like a _____.
O	19. ORNITHOPTER	S.	He talks like a dictionary and sits on Max's shoulders
Y	20. SHOULDERS	T.	Killer Kane's plea before going to trial
C	21. PURSE	U.	Kevin's doctor
W	22. LORETTA	V.	What Max didn't have until Freak came along.
Q	23. CRETIN	W.	Heroic Biker Babe
V	24. BRAIN	X.	Loretta and Iggy live in the New _____
G	25. ICU	Y.	Freak sits on Max's

MATCHING 2 - Freak the Mighty

1. PHILBRICK
2. HERO
3. REMEMBERING
4. SEIZURE
5. HIM
6. GUINEVERE
7. PREACHER
8. FREAK
9. BIONIC
10. WHISTLES
11. KANE
12. MAX
13. GRAM
14. CRETIN
15. READ
16. TESTAMENTS
17. INSIDE
18. DICTIONARY
19. BOOK
20. KNIGHTS
21. PAROLE
22. IGGY
23. LORETTA
24. ARTHUR
25. SULFURIC

A. King ___, once a wimpy little kid, an orphan who pulled a sword from the stone
B. How Freak gets the cops attention
C. Heroic Biker Babe
D. What Freak calls Tony D
E. Killer Kane violated his
F. First human version of robots, according to Freak
G. What the police call Max for saving Kevin
H. Author of Freak the Mighty
I. Max's grandmother
J. Boss of the Panheads
K. Freak grew on the ____ but not on the outside
L. One of the names Kevin uses for his mother
M. Max's father
N. Freak gives Max a blank one and tells him to fill it with their adventures.
O. The Mighty part of Freak the Mighty
P. Freak writes one for Max
Q. Killer____: Max's father
R. Freak sprays Killer Kane in the eyes with fake _____ acid.
S. The Experimental _____ Unit: where Freak will become the first bionically improved human
T. _____ is just an invention of the mind.
U. What happens to Freak on his birthday
V. He talks like a dictionary and sits on Max's shoulders
W. Freak taught Max how to do this better
X. Loretta and Iggy live in the New _____
Y. Killer Kane planned to become one to get money

MATCHING 2 ANSWER KEY - Freak the Mighty

H	1. PHILBRICK	A.	King ___, once a wimpy little kid, an orphan who pulled a sword from the stone
G	2. HERO	B.	How Freak gets the cops attention
T	3. REMEMBERING	C.	Heroic Biker Babe
U	4. SEIZURE	D.	What Freak calls Tony D
M	5. HIM	E.	Killer Kane violated his
L	6. GUINEVERE	F.	First human version of robots, according to Freak
Y	7. PREACHER	G.	What the police call Max for saving Kevin
V	8. FREAK	H.	Author of Freak the Mighty
S	9. BIONIC	I.	Max's grandmother
B	10. WHISTLES	J.	Boss of the Panheads
Q	11. KANE	K.	Freak grew on the ___ but not on the outside
O	12. MAX	L.	One of the names Kevin uses for his mother
I	13. GRAM	M.	Max's father
D	14. CRETIN	N.	Freak gives Max a blank one and tells him to fill it with their adventures.
W	15. READ	O.	The Mighty part of Freak the Mighty
X	16. TESTAMENTS	P.	Freak writes one for Max
K	17. INSIDE	Q.	Killer___: Max's father
P	18. DICTIONARY	R.	Freak sprays Killer Kane in the eyes with fake ___ acid.
N	19. BOOK	S.	The Experimental ___ Unit: where Freak will become the first bionically improved human
F	20. KNIGHTS	T.	___ is just an invention of the mind.
E	21. PAROLE	U.	What happens to Freak on his birthday
J	22. IGGY	V.	He talks like a dictionary and sits on Max's shoulders
C	23. LORETTA	W.	Freak taught Max how to do this better
A	24. ARTHUR	X.	Loretta and Iggy live in the New ___
R	25. SULFURIC	Y.	Killer Kane planned to become one to get money

JUGGLE LETTERS 1 - Freak the Mighty

_____ = 1. BEIALCXUR

King Arthur's magical sword

_____ = 2. CRPEHEAR

Killer Kane planned to become one to get money

_____ = 3. ITNECR

What Freak calls Tony D

_____ = 4. CIU

Where Freak dies

_____ = 5. IEDLLON

Sends Max and Freak to the principals office

_____ = 6. FIEL

____ is dangerous.

_____ = 7. RSNTGLAE

Killer Kane's method of killing

_____ = 8. IHNTGKS

First human version of robots, according to Freak

_____ = 9. FEKRA

He talks like a dictionary and sits on Max's shoulders

_____ =10. DBELA

Tony D's nickname

_____ =11. RIBNA

What Max didn't have until Freak came along.

_____ =12. GIYG

Boss of the Panheads

_____ =13. DSEHLRUOS

Freak sits on Max's

_____ =14. MRIG

He built the Down Under.

JUGGLE LETTERS 1 ANSWER KEY - Freak the Mighty

EXCALIBUR = 1. BEIALCXUR
King Arthur's magical sword

PREACHER = 2. CRPEHEAR
Killer Kane planned to become one to get money

CRETIN = 3. ITNECR
What Freak calls Tony D

ICU = 4. CIU
Where Freak dies

DONELLI = 5. IEDLLON
Sends Max and Freak to the principals office

LIFE = 6. FIEL
____ is dangerous.

STRANGLE = 7. RSNTGLAE
Killer Kane's method of killing

KNIGHTS = 8. IHNTGKS
First human version of robots, according to Freak

FREAK = 9. FEKRA
He talks like a dictionary and sits on Max's shoulders

BLADE =10. DBELA
Tony D's nickname

BRAIN =11. RIBNA
What Max didn't have until Freak came along.

IGGY =12. GIYG
Boss of the Panheads

SHOULDERS =13. DSEHLRUOS
Freak sits on Max's

GRIM =14. MRIG
He built the Down Under.

JUGGLE LETTERS 2 - Freak the Mighty

_____ = 1. PAVIKS

Kevin's doctor

_____ = 2. MIH

Max's father

_____ = 3. EOHR

What the police call Max for saving Kevin

_____ = 4. IELF

____ is dangerous.

_____ = 5. SWELSTHI

How Freak gets the cops attention

_____ = 6. DERA

Freak taught Max how to do this better

_____ = 7. AYPIRDM

Max's Christmas present from Freak is in a box shaped like a _____.

_____ = 8. EZIUERS

What happens to Freak on his birthday

_____ = 9. WGNE

Friend of Max's mother

_____ =10. ARNTIYCIDO

Freak writes one for Max

_____ =11. LUYGIT

Killer Kane's plea before going to trial

_____ =12. UHOSDRELS

Freak sits on Max's

_____ =13. REALTOT

Heroic Biker Babe

_____ =14. CETHAARCR

Grim is concerned Max will inherit this from his father

JUGGLE LETTERS 2 ANSWER KEY - Freak the Mighty

SPIVAK	= 1.	PAVIKS
		Kevin's doctor
HIM	= 2.	MIH
		Max's father
HERO	= 3.	EOHR
		What the police call Max for saving Kevin
LIFE	= 4.	IELF
		____ is dangerous.
WHISTLES	= 5.	SWELSTHI
		How Freak gets the cops attention
READ	= 6.	DERA
		Freak taught Max how to do this better
PYRAMID	= 7.	AYPIRDM
		Max's Christmas present from Freak is in a box shaped like a ____.
SEIZURE	= 8.	EZIUERS
		What happens to Freak on his birthday
GWEN	= 9.	WGNE
		Friend of Max's mother
DICTIONARY	=10.	ARNTIYCIDO
		Freak writes one for Max
GUILTY	=11.	LUYGIT
		Killer Kane's plea before going to trial
SHOULDERS	=12.	UHOSDRELS
		Freak sits on Max's
LORETTA	=13.	REALTOT
		Heroic Biker Babe
CHARACTER	=14.	CETHAARCR
		Grim is concerned Max will inherit this from his father

VOCABULARY RESOURCE MATERIALS

Freak the Mighty Vocabulary Word List

ABDUCT	Take (someone) away illegally by force or deception
ABERRATION	Unwelcome deviation from normal
ACCOMMODATIONS	Living space; lodgings
ALTERNATIVES	Choices
ARCHETYPE	An original model
AUTOMATIC	Working by itself with little or no direct human control
CAMOUFLAGE	Protective coloring or disguise
CONSEQUENCES	Results of one's actions
CONVERGING	Coming together in one place
CORROSIVE	Capable of destroying slowly by chemical action
DELIGHTED	Very happy
DEMEANOR	The way a person behaves
DETENTION	Punishment of being kept in school after hours
DIVULGED	Made known; revealed
DYSFUNCTIONAL	Not operating normally or properly
DYSLEXIC	Having difficulty interpreting words, letters, and symbols
EMBARRASSED	To feel self-conscious or ill at ease
ESPECIALLY	To a great degree; very much
EVASIVE	Tending or intended to avoid
EXPEL	Eject forcefully
EXPRESSION	Word or phrase communicating an idea
FACILITATE	Make easier
FEALTY	Loyalty; faithfulness
FIERCE	Violent or aggressive: ferocious
FRANTIC	Conducted in a hurried and chaotic way; full of fear or anxiety
FUNCTIONAL	Useful; practical; working
FURROWED	Trenched; rutted; grooved; wrinkled
HOODLUM	Tough and aggressive young man
HYPNOTIZED	Put into a trance
IGNORANT	Lacking knowledge
INJUSTICE	Something unfair and wrong
INTENSIVE	Concentrated; thorough
INTERVENTION	Action taken to improve a medical disorder
INVENTION	Something newly created
MANIFESTATION	Object that shows or embodies something
MIRACULOUS	Like a miracle; happening without any natural or scientific explanation
MORON	Stupid person
OATH	Solemn promise
OBLIGATION	Duty
OBNOXIOUS	Extremely unpleasant
OPTIMUM	Most favorable; best
PARALYZED	Caused to be incapable of movement

Freak the Mighty Vocabulary Word List continued

PARTICULAR	Specific; a certain one
PERSPECTIVE	A view or outlook
PHONY	Fake
POSSESSED	Controlled as if by a spirit or other force
PRECAUTION	Measure taken in advance to prevent something undesirable from happening
PRECIOUS	Valuable; having great value
PRODIGY	Young person with exceptional abilities
PROPULSION	Force that sends forward
PYRAMID	Structure with a square or triangular base and sloping sides that meet in a point at the top
REGURGITATE	To vomit
REMARKABLE	Uncommon; worthy of notice
RETRIEVAL	Act or process of getting something back
RINGER	Informal term for a person's double
SCUTTLE	Run hurriedly with short quick steps
SOBRIQUET	Nickname
STABILIZED	Balanced; made less likely to fall
STEED	Horse
TELEMETRY	Transmission of readings to a distant receiving set or station
TEMPORARY	Not lasting
TENEMENTS	Apartment houses over-crowded and poorly maintained
TRACHEOTOMY	Incision in the windpipe made to relieve an obstruction to breathing
TRAJECTORY	The path of a moving body or particle
TROUSERS	Pants
TRUSSED	Tied up
UNIQUE	One of a kind
URGENCY	Need for immediate attention or action
VIOLATE	Break or fail to comply with a rule or agreement

VOCABULARY WORD SEARCH - Freak the Mighty

```
S S Z R R E L H F Q U C A M O U F L A G E
R C T Y V T X B C R P N T N M P U L E N L
E V A S I V E P P A A I I J N O R C L O R
S M F C O N V E R G I N G Q P Y R A M I D
U L B A T N J T E E Q J T O U E O O N T Q
O A T A Y Z I M C V S U S I I E W G N N G
R H R N R C F R I N W S D F C Q E P B E N
T I O C U R O V O R E T I I S R D T P V O
P H N L H N A I U S T I V O V T J R I R B
P A A V A E T S S Y X C C S N U E O X E N
C R R E E N T E S T P E Y E M C L E W T O
P O M A E N D Y E E M Q V T A A A G D N X
D E N T L L T U P N D I S U T R N M E I I
D E E S L Y Q I O E S P T E S E O I T D O
A D L W E I Z I O N K I N V C M I R E E U
B D P I R Q T E E N O Y E I U A T A L Z S
D K Y B G A U T D N J T M S T R C C E I M
U L O S R H N E X P E L E O T K N U M T D
C S P R L I T K N D F A N R L A U L E O E
T V E M Z E F E V C T E E R E B F O T N S
B B P R X X X S D T T E F T O N L T U R P S
A J R P R O D I G Y P S X C Q E J S Y Y U
N G N U R G E N C Y H O O D L U M C M H R
D Y S F U N C T I O N A L I G N O R A N T
```

ABDUCT	EVASIVE	INVENTION	RINGER
ABERRATION	EXPEL	MIRACULOUS	SCUTTLE
ARCHETYPE	EXPRESSION	MORON	SOBRIQUET
CAMOUFLAGE	FEALTY	OATH	STEED
CONSEQUENCES	FIERCE	OBNOXIOUS	TELEMETRY
CONVERGING	FRANTIC	PARALYZED	TENEMENTS
CORROSIVE	FUNCTIONAL	PARTICULAR	TROUSERS
DELIGHTED	FURROWED	PHONY	TRUSSED
DEMEANOR	HOODLUM	POSSESSED	UNIQUE
DETENTION	HYPNOTIZED	PRECAUTION	URGENCY
DIVULGED	IGNORANT	PRECIOUS	VIOLATE
DYSFUNCTIONAL	INJUSTICE	PRODIGY	
DYSLEXIC	INTENSIVE	PYRAMID	
EMBARRASSED	INTERVENTION	REMARKABLE	

VOCABULARY WORD SEARCH ANSWER KEY - Freak the Mighty

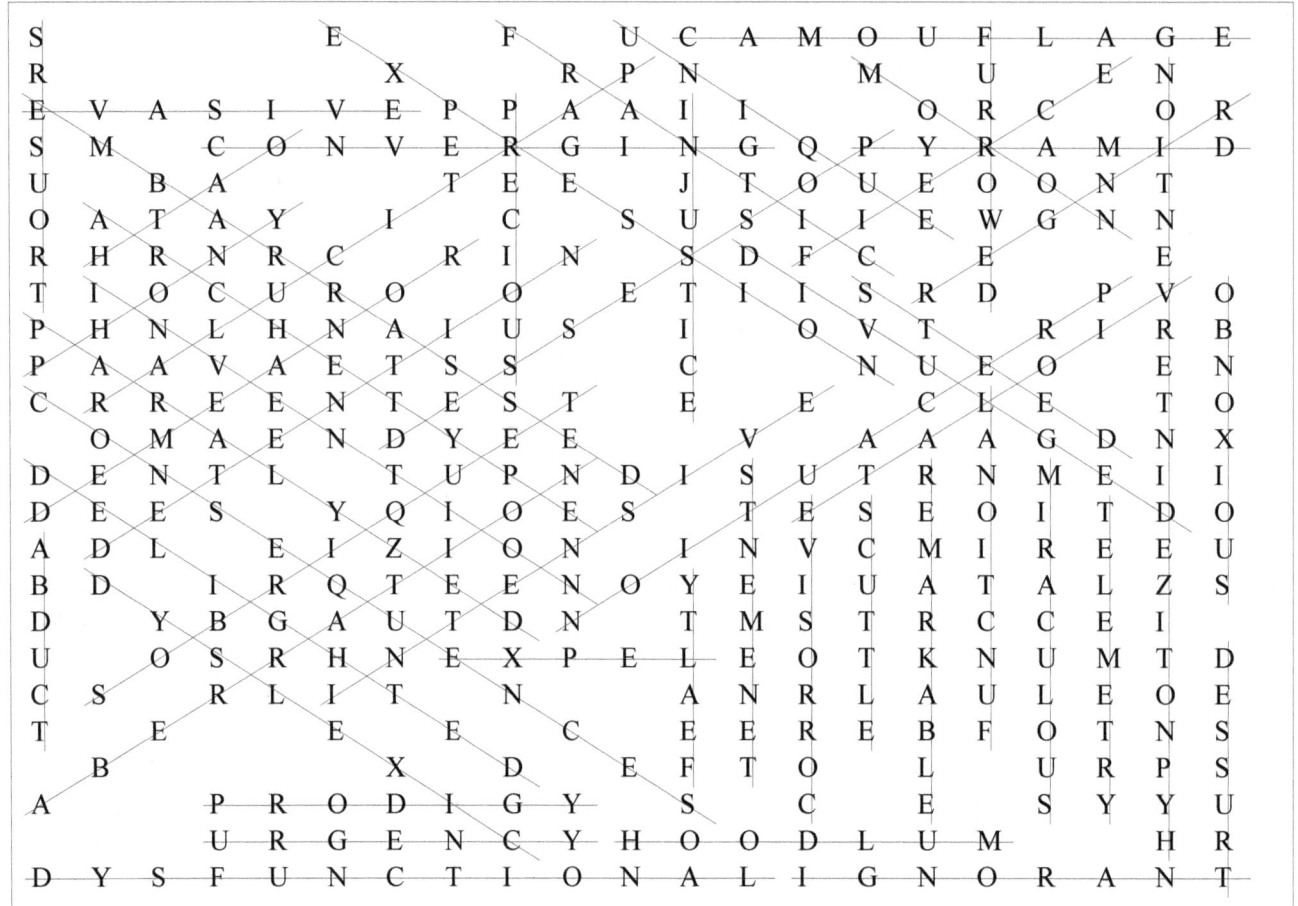

ABDUCT	EVASIVE	INVENTION	RINGER
ABERRATION	EXPEL	MIRACULOUS	SCUTTLE
ARCHETYPE	EXPRESSION	MORON	SOBRIQUET
CAMOUFLAGE	FEALTY	OATH	STEED
CONSEQUENCES	FIERCE	OBNOXIOUS	TELEMETRY
CONVERGING	FRANTIC	PARALYZED	TENEMENTS
CORROSIVE	FUNCTIONAL	PARTICULAR	TROUSERS
DELIGHTED	FURROWED	PHONY	TRUSSED
DEMEANOR	HOODLUM	POSSESSED	UNIQUE
DETENTION	HYPNOTIZED	PRECAUTION	URGENCY
DIVULGED	IGNORANT	PRECIOUS	VIOLATE
DYSFUNCTIONAL	INJUSTICE	PRODIGY	
DYSLEXIC	INTENSIVE	PYRAMID	
EMBARRASSED	INTERVENTION	REMARKABLE	

VOCABULARY CROSSWORD - Freak the Mighty

Across
1. Make easier
2. Stupid person
5. Very happy
8. Run hurriedly with short, quick steps
12. Living space; lodgings
13. Loyalty; faithfulness
15. Take (someone) away illegally by force or deception
16. Horse
18. Most favorable; best
19. Informal term for a person's double
20. Break or fail to comply with a rule or agreement

Down
1. Violent or aggressive: ferocious
3. Solemn promise
4. Duty
6. Tough and aggressive young man
7. Tending or intended to avoid
9. Results of one's actions
10. Made known; revealed
11. Choices
12. Unwelcome deviation from normal
13. Conducted in a hurried and chaotic way; full of fear or anxiety
14. Something unfair and wrong
17. Eject forcefully

VOCABULARY CROSSWORD ANSWER KEY - Freak the Mighty

		1 F	A	C	I	L	I	T	A	T	E		2 M	3 O	R	4 O	N
		I												A		B	
	5 D	E	L	I	6 G	H	7 T	E	D		8 S	9 C	U	T	T	L	E
		R			O		V		10 D		O		H		I		11 A
12 A	C	C	O	M	M	O	D	A	T	I	O	N	S		13 F	E	A	L	T	Y
B		E			D		S		I		V		S		F	E	A	L	T	Y
E			14 I		L		I		U		E		R		T		E
R			N		U		V		L		Q		A		I		R
R			J		M		E		G		U		N		O		N
15 A	B	D	U	C	T				E		E		T		N		A
T			S			16 S	T	17 E	E	D		N		I			T
I			T					X				C		C			I
18 O	P	T	I	M	U	M		P				E					V
N			C					E				S		19 R	I	N	G	E	R
			E	20 V	I	O	L	A	T	E							S

Across
1. Make easier
2. Stupid person
5. Very happy
8. Run hurriedly with short, quick steps
12. Living space; lodgings
13. Loyalty; faithfulness
15. Take (someone) away illegally by force or deception
16. Horse
18. Most favorable; best
19. Informal term for a person's double
20. Break or fail to comply with a rule or agreement

Down
1. Violent or aggressive: ferocious
3. Solemn promise
4. Duty
6. Tough and aggressive young man
7. Tending or intended to avoid
9. Results of one's actions
10. Made known; revealed
11. Choices
12. Unwelcome deviation from normal
13. Conducted in a hurried and chaotic way; full of fear or anxiety
14. Something unfair and wrong
17. Eject forcefully

VOCABULARY MATCHING 1 - Freak the Mighty

1. INTENSIVE
2. MIRACULOUS
3. EXPEL
4. TRUSSED
5. POSSESSED
6. OBLIGATION
7. FACILITATE
8. TEMPORARY
9. HOODLUM
10. FRANTIC
11. PYRAMID
12. DEMEANOR
13. PERSPECTIVE
14. DIVULGED
15. TRACHEOTOMY
16. TENEMENTS
17. INVENTION
18. EMBARRASSED
19. REGURGITATE
20. CONSEQUENCES
21. CONVERGING
22. ARCHETYPE
23. PARALYZED
24. OPTIMUM
25. DYSLEXIC

A. Structure with a square or triangular base and sloping sides that meet in a point at the top
B. Something newly created
C. Duty
D. To feel self-conscious or ill at ease
E. Eject forcefully
F. Most favorable; best
G. Made known; revealed
H. Incision in the windpipe made to relieve an obstruction to breathing
I. Coming together in one place
J. Like a miracle; happening without any natural or scientific explanation
K. To vomit
L. An original model
M. Results of one's actions
N. Tied up
O. Not lasting
P. The way a person behaves
Q. A view or outlook
R. Tough and aggressive young man
S. Conducted in a hurried and chaotic way; full of fear or anxiety
T. Apartment houses over-crowed and poorly maintained
U. Caused to be incapable of movement
V. Make easier
W. Concentrated; thorough
X. Controlled as if by a spirit or other force
Y. Having difficulty interpreting words, letters, and symbols

VOCABULARY MATCHING 1 ANSWER KEY - Freak the Mighty

W	1. INTENSIVE	A.	Structure with a square or triangular base and sloping sides that meet in a point at the top
J	2. MIRACULOUS	B.	Something newly created
E	3. EXPEL	C.	Duty
N	4. TRUSSED	D.	To feel self-conscious or ill at ease
X	5. POSSESSED	E.	Eject forcefully
C	6. OBLIGATION	F.	Most favorable; best
V	7. FACILITATE	G.	Made known; revealed
O	8. TEMPORARY	H.	Incision in the windpipe made to relieve an obstruction to breathing
R	9. HOODLUM	I.	Coming together in one place
S	10. FRANTIC	J.	Like a miracle; happening without any natural or scientific explanation
A	11. PYRAMID	K.	To vomit
P	12. DEMEANOR	L.	An original model
Q	13. PERSPECTIVE	M.	Results of one's actions
G	14. DIVULGED	N.	Tied up
H	15. TRACHEOTOMY	O.	Not lasting
T	16. TENEMENTS	P.	The way a person behaves
B	17. INVENTION	Q.	A view or outlook
D	18. EMBARRASSED	R.	Tough and aggressive young man
K	19. REGURGITATE	S.	Conducted in a hurried and chaotic way; full of fear or anxiety
M	20. CONSEQUENCES	T.	Apartment houses over-crowded and poorly maintained
I	21. CONVERGING	U.	Caused to be incapable of movement
L	22. ARCHETYPE	V.	Make easier
U	23. PARALYZED	W.	Concentrated; thorough
F	24. OPTIMUM	X.	Controlled as if by a spirit or other force
Y	25. DYSLEXIC	Y.	Having difficulty interpreting words, letters, and symbols

VOCABULARY MATCHING 2 - Freak the Mighty

1. RETRIEVAL — A. Transmission of readings to a distant receiving set or station
2. TELEMETRY — B. Trenched; rutted; grooved; wrinkled
3. ALTERNATIVES — C. Living space; lodgings
4. FEALTY — D. Loyalty; faithfulness
5. ARCHETYPE — E. Made known; revealed
6. DIVULGED — F. To feel self-conscious or ill at ease
7. HYPNOTIZED — G. Something newly created
8. INJUSTICE — H. Concentrated; thorough
9. CAMOUFLAGE — I. Duty
10. TENEMENTS — J. Tough and aggressive young man
11. PARALYZED — K. Informal term for a person's double
12. ACCOMMODATIONS — L. A view or outlook
13. EMBARRASSED — M. Apartment houses over-crowded and poorly maintained
14. PRODIGY — N. Very happy
15. HOODLUM — O. Choices
16. PERSPECTIVE — P. Working by itself with little or no direct human control
17. INTENSIVE — Q. Caused to be incapable of movement
18. SCUTTLE — R. Having difficulty interpreting words, letters, and symbols
19. AUTOMATIC — S. Something unfair and wrong
20. RINGER — T. Act or process of getting something back
21. DYSLEXIC — U. Run hurriedly with short, quick steps
22. OBLIGATION — V. Put into a trance
23. DELIGHTED — W. Young person with exceptional abilities
24. INVENTION — X. An original model
25. FURROWED — Y. Protective coloring or disguise

VOCABULARY MATCHING 2 ANSWER KEY - Freak the Mighty

T	1. RETRIEVAL	A.	Transmission of readings to a distant receiving set or station
A	2. TELEMETRY	B.	Trenched; rutted; grooved; wrinkled
O	3. ALTERNATIVES	C.	Living space; lodgings
D	4. FEALTY	D.	Loyalty; faithfulness
X	5. ARCHETYPE	E.	Made known; revealed
E	6. DIVULGED	F.	To feel self-conscious or ill at ease
V	7. HYPNOTIZED	G.	Something newly created
S	8. INJUSTICE	H.	Concentrated; thorough
Y	9. CAMOUFLAGE	I.	Duty
M	10. TENEMENTS	J.	Tough and aggressive young man
Q	11. PARALYZED	K.	Informal term for a person's double
C	12. ACCOMMODATIONS	L.	A view or outlook
F	13. EMBARRASSED	M.	Apartment houses over-crowed and poorly maintained
W	14. PRODIGY	N.	Very happy
J	15. HOODLUM	O.	Choices
L	16. PERSPECTIVE	P.	Working by itself with little or no direct human control
H	17. INTENSIVE	Q.	Caused to be incapable of movement
U	18. SCUTTLE	R.	Having difficulty interpreting words, letters, and symbols
P	19. AUTOMATIC	S.	Something unfair and wrong
K	20. RINGER	T.	Act or process of getting something back
R	21. DYSLEXIC	U.	Run hurriedly with short, quick steps
I	22. OBLIGATION	V.	Put into a trance
N	23. DELIGHTED	W.	Young person with exceptional abilities
G	24. INVENTION	X.	An original model
B	25. FURROWED	Y.	Protective coloring or disguise

VOCABULARY JUGGLE LETTERS 1 - Freak the Mighty

_____ = 1. DETES

Horse

_____ = 2. AMICTOUTA

Working by itself with little or no direct human control

_____ = 3. QOSETBIUR

Nickname

_____ = 4. RIPESUOC

Valuable; having great value

_____ = 5. RRGTETAIEUG

To vomit

_____ = 6. ZSITIBDLAE

Balanced; made less likely to fall

_____ = 7. CAPHRTEYE

An original model

_____ = 8. AIOADSMNOTOCCM

Living space; lodgings

_____ = 9. IEECRF

Violent or aggressive: ferocious

_____ =10. NPYDETIOZH

Put into a trance

_____ =11. NUEYRGC

Need for immediate attention or action

_____ =12. MIPOMUT

Most favorable; best

_____ =13. REIGRN

Informal term for a person's double

_____ =14. EYAEILPCSL

To a great degree; very much

VOCABULARY JUGGLE LETTERS 1 ANSWER KEY - Freak the Mighty

STEED = 1. DETES
Horse

AUTOMATIC = 2. AMICTOUTA
Working by itself with little or no direct human control

SOBRIQUET = 3. QOSETBIUR
Nickname

PRECIOUS = 4. RIPESUOC
Valuable; having great value

REGURGITATE = 5. RRGTETAIEUG
To vomit

STABILIZED = 6. ZSITIBDLAE
Balanced; made less likely to fall

ARCHETYPE = 7. CAPHRTEYE
An original model

ACCOMMODATIONS = 8. AIOADSMNOTOCCM
Living space; lodgings

FIERCE = 9. IEECRF
Violent or aggressive: ferocious

HYPNOTIZED = 10. NPYDETIOZH
Put into a trance

URGENCY = 11. NUEYRGC
Need for immediate attention or action

OPTIMUM = 12. MIPOMUT
Most favorable; best

RINGER = 13. REIGRN
Informal term for a person's double

ESPECIALLY = 14. EYAEILPCSL
To a great degree; very much

VOCABULARY JUGGLE LETTERS 2 - Freak the Mighty

= 1. LEVREATIR

   Act or process of getting something back

= 2. DEDEGTLIH

   Very happy

= 3. STTAVLIRNAEE

   Choices

= 4. NEVNONTII

   Something newly created

= 5. AICRPOTUEN

   Measure taken in advance to prevent something undesirable from happening

= 6. EECFIR

   Violent or aggressive: ferocious

= 7. EESDT

   Horse

= 8. VUGDEDLI

   Made known; revealed

= 9. UCTBDA

   Take (someone) away illegally by force or deception

=10. NAOIMASINFTET

   Object that shows or embodies something

=11. THAO

   Solemn promise

=12. MOAICNADSMTOOC

   Living space; lodgings

=13. RROEATBANI

   Unwelcome deviation from normal

=14. OERUWFRD

   Trenched; rutted; grooved; wrinkled

VOCABULARY JUGGLE LETTERS 2 ANSWER KEY - Freak the Mighty

RETRIEVAL = 1. LEVREATIR

Act or process of getting something back

DELIGHTED = 2. DEDEGTLIH

Very happy

ALTERNATIVES = 3. STTAVLIRNAEE

Choices

INVENTION = 4. NEVNONTII

Something newly created

PRECAUTION = 5. AICRPOTUEN

Measure taken in advance to prevent something undesirable from happening

FIERCE = 6. EECFIR

Violent or aggressive: ferocious

STEED = 7. EESDT

Horse

DIVULGED = 8. VUGDEDLI

Made known; revealed

ABDUCT = 9. UCTBDA

Take (someone) away illegally by force or deception

MANIFESTATION =10. NAOIMASINFTET

Object that shows or embodies something

OATH =11. THAO

Solemn promise

ACCOMMODATIONS =12. MOAICNADSMTOOC

Living space; lodgings

ABERRATION =13. RROEATBANI

Unwelcome deviation from normal

FURROWED =14. OERUWFRD

Trenched; rutted; grooved; wrinkled

www.ingramcontent.com/pod-product-compliance
Lightning Source LLC
LaVergne TN
LVHW081533060526
838200LV00048B/2074